Transforming Mother Wound

Sacred Pathways for the Wild & Sovereign

Monika Carless

Earth Spirit Press
Vancouver Island, Canada

Copyright © 2022 **Monika Carless/Earth Spirit Press**
Cover Art and Interior Drawings © 2021 **Angie Shea**
Interior Design/Editing by **Ashley Jane Aesthetics**

For more information on the author, visit monikacarless.com.

Transforming Mother Wound: Sacred Pathways for the Wild & Sovereign
/Monika Carless
1ˢᵗ Edition 2022
ISBN: 978-0-9869193-3-6

Contents

*"The things that women reclaim are often their own voice,
their own values, their imagination, their clairvoyance,
their stories, their ancient memories. If we go for the
deeper, and the darker, and the less known,
we will touch the bones."*

Clarissa Pinkola Estés

"As long as we resist the pain or the truth – the heart healing, and therefore the light, which so many desire to enter – is blocked.

And we stay stuck in things that aren't our true self, our highest good, sometimes only to avoid a few moments of 'truth'.

Start where you are.

Don't reschedule change.

Move with what's possible."

Sophie Gregoire – She is the Moon

Surrendering to the Sacred Womb of Healing

I am so very honored to share with you a map for finding peace with the story of your mother wound. If you are here, your soul has called you to this work.

This is a dynamic exploration focused on transformation at a cellular, inter-generational level with interactive pages that invite you to participate in your healing journey.

Through this journey, you may find that your creativity, intuition, soul-frequency, empathy, connection to yourself, Source and all life forms is deepened.

Embodied and aligned, your body, mind, and spirit will embark on a new path... one of embracing the medicine of past wounds and becoming fearlessly oneself.

The Ancients valued the natural rhythms of the Universe and planet, and in this way, found rootedness in their humanity as well as the sacredness of their infinite natures.

It is in our humanity that we experience all there is – the light, the dark, the inner world, and the outer. All is sacred. You are sacred.

In this work, I undertook to honor the mystery, magic, and the unseen elements of transforming core wounding, because life is so much more than what can be quantified through linear science. It is also your multi-dimensionality, your humanity, and spirituality. Let us explore together.

With Love,
Monika

The template for healing mother wound is the template we can use for healing all wounds, because it teaches us to be in harmony with what is, and with ourselves.

My experience with Mother Wound has been one of the greatest lessons of my life.

Writing this book has been my act of devotion to the Consciousness and service to humanity.

I am honored to be part of your rising, Beloved, as others have been part of mine.

It has been an undeniable spiritual initiation to have been on the journey of orphanhood, adoption, relocation, challenge, and eventually awakening to my purpose. I offer my story, my process, and my gratitude through these pages, created for the collective healing of Mother Wound and the Great Mother Herself.

I have always looked for the root of things because that is where the story of anything begins and where it is best understood.

The winding road of healing took me deep into the woods, into something I remembered faintly, until I emerged a witch, a soul-alchemist.

Three long distance pilgrimages across the wilds of Northern England brought remembrance of past lives, connecting with ancient memories of the Divine Feminine and my ancestral roots. I expanded into holistic nutrition, organic farming, and local food initiatives. Each step taken, although sometimes seemingly random, came with a deeper understanding of myself, of my place in the world, of the incredible synchronicity of my life, the wisdom of my wounding, and what I was here to do.

Simultaneously, I grew two free-range daughters, encouraging free-thought, un-schooling them at times, always seeking to not repeat the cycle of my turbulent childhood, with well-intentioned but mixed results. They grew, and I grew, realizing in the process that my mother (much like I) had been nursing her own core wounds.

Words and writing became the ultimate medicine for my own mother wound and the portal for this work.

I am the clear channel of the soul-group 'Aiden'. I am the author of over 350 published articles and The Dark Pool Trilogy, a foray into conscious relationships, spiritual manna, sacred sexuality, and the union of the mature feminine and masculine.

As an initiate of the Munay-Ki Rites, I found direct paths to shedding the skin of core wounds and am honored to pass these teachings on to my community. My life and potent rise from the proverbial ashes of mother wound is now the soil of my teachings.

Healing Mother Wound is what the whole village needs.

Creating Safe Ground

We dance with mother wound to find our worth and purpose. Mother may never actualize into the person we think we need her to be; and yet, we can become our own center. The fact is, we have exactly the right mother to launch us on our wisdom path. She is the portal for our empowerment. Mother is our awakening.

A Call to Circle

Mother Wound is a portal through which we walk to awaken unconditional love and compassion within our hearts. I witness your courage and your determination for understanding and healing at such a profound level.

Imagine that in reading this book, you are joining a circle of sisters at a round table, each of us with equal voice and presence. Women around the world are participating in healing their mother wound, and you are united through intention. The symbolism of the circle is as infinity itself, a cosmic mystery whose energy holds the codes of everything that is. To sit in the circle is to be part of Womb space, to embrace the cyclical nature of life. It is Unity and Inclusion, Wholeness and Completion. It is Centering.

As part of my dedication and service to you, I cast a magical circle inviting the elements of Air, Water, Earth, Fire, and the Four Directions to your work.

I invite and thank all the spirits and Goddesses with whom you resonate to join you. I ask the wisdom of your Ancestors to guide you and call for the temple of your heart to open to what is ahead. May you be embraced by the warmth and safety of this circle.

And so, it is…

Queen, Mother, Daughter, Wise Woman,
Lover, Teacher, Maiden, Crone

The archetypes of the Divine Feminine
express themselves in many ways.

She is not to be contained,
a wildfire that consumes and nourishes, births, and heals.
She is at times a raging river,
other times a silent breeze.

She dances with her guides, ancestors, and angels.
Boundless. Erotic. Wise. Surrendered. Receptive.

The Sacred Pathway to Healing Core Wounds

We find our own way, don't we?
Our way is as unique as we are, and there is no time limit set for transformation. And yet, there are certain tangible steps we can choose in order to find acceptance and peace, surrender and empowerment.

UNDERSTAND THAT NONE OF IT WAS YOUR FAULT

Practice compassion, loving kindness, and forgiveness towards yourself.

KNOW YOURSELF

When you understand your own mystery, your purpose, and your soul mission, you can step bravely into your empowerment with your story as fuel for wisdom.

SEE MOTHER FOR WHO SHE IS, INSTEAD OF THE WOMAN YOU'D LIKE HER TO BE

Mother is a complex archetype and thought form. Let go of expectations and see mother as woman first, systemically programmed within a patriarchal world.

GRIEVE THE ABSENT MOTHER AND THE WOUNDED CHILD

Allow space for grief and release of big emotions. Support your inner child.

Witness and be Present to Your Wounding, Emotions, and Experiences

Look at what happened honestly and with presence. Witness the pain, and it will witness itself. Fear and anger have a place to express themselves and dissipate.

Find Your Inner Mother – Self-Soothe

Taking responsibility for our own life experience, finding ways to nurture ourselves, and shedding the skin of wounding helps us to manifest the life that we want, release mother from her role as the perpetrator, and cease seeking a 'rescuer' relationship, moving from co-dependence to co-creation.

Build Strong Boundaries

Healthy and strong boundaries with others, and with yourself, protect you from repeating the cycles of abuse, abandonment, and neglect.

Find Support

Seek out supportive relationships with positive people. Find therapy as needed. Avoid drama. Nurture your relationship with Great Mother.

Know That Healing is a Spiral

Healing from mother wound is not a destination; it is a journey of self-discovery and is like any natural cycle...we return time and again to learn deeper truths, surrender to the process, and grow in wisdom.

At the beginning of our journey to healing, we awaken to our conditioned self: the one who moves in comfortable and predictable patterns and reactions. We witness this conditioned self with a desire for change. To meet ourselves in this way is challenging. At first, like during stages of grief, we may experience shock and shame.

In the next stage of healing, we become conscious of how we actually co-create our life, that we are not victims of some mysterious fate, but that we can consciously create our own reality. The conditioned self dissolves some more, taking intentional steps.

Later, we meet with grief and the Inner Child whose life experiences are those of the individual and the collective.

Through the process, we meet surrender – to what was, what is, and what we are creating. As we love ourselves more deeply, with grounded compassion and grace, an acceptance is born.

We live on a deeper level, in a more authentic dimension, where the trauma or wound becomes the gift, serving us and others.

EVIDENCE OF HEALING

- Feeling at home and safe in your body and in the world.
- Holding memories with courage, love, and compassion instead of fearing them.
- Accepting your mind and thoughts as allies.
- Consistently living in the present moment.

*As much as we are individuals, we are also part of a clan.
Like wolves, women intuitively understand that
connections keep us safe, alive, and in tune with the
greater world.*

Understanding Trauma

- Trauma happens when the nervous system is overwhelmed by an experience. It can be brought on by violence, war, attack, accident, verbal or emotional abuse, childhood trauma, shock of witnessing trauma, etc.
- Some of the symptoms of trauma are anger, anxiety, fear, depression, physical manifestations, withdrawal, and thoughts of self-harm.
- Trauma is furthered when one's trauma is not acknowledged.
- One may get stuck in any of three stages of trauma: the original shock, the orientation stage (trying to make sense of it), or the initial response to the trauma.

ASSISTED/SELF-HEALING CONSISTS OF SEVERAL STEPS:

- **Creating safe space to explore the trauma**. This includes gathering resources and tools to use along the journey. Resources can be somatic practices, relationships, attitudes, habits, conditions, and/or qualities.

  What can help me walk these shadows and stay grounded and stable while I do so?

- **Exploring the trauma**. How does it feel in my body? What do I remember, sense, know, intuit? The trauma may have a size, shape, smell, sound, or color associated with it.

- **Identifying** how one could be in relationship to the trauma that would build resilience, safety, and positive outcomes. Practicing loving-kindness towards oneself.

  What can you do now that you could not do before when faced with the memories?

- **Distinguishing** between healthy and unhealthy responses. Pulling in more resources.

- **Releasing** trauma from the body and recognizing one's resilience and courage.

- **Integrating** the experience by embodying creative ways to explore and process trauma resulting in feelings of self-worth, strength, and peace.

First Steps

"And if we rise up rooted...like trees, well then, women might indeed save not only themselves but the world"

Sharon Blackie

Journal Creation

The inner work stemming from these pages may be recorded in the journal that goes with this book or one of your choosing.

It can be filled with your words, art, magazine clippings, pen, colored pencil or markers, photographs, or colored yarn. Allow your creativity to play. An online journal is another alternative, although I encourage one in the physical realm so that you can 'hold' your journey in your hands.

Creativity is an inherent part of the Divine Feminine. This is an excellent way to connect with our own identity as the I Am/Source.

Your Goddess Image

Flowing further, I invite you to take a photograph of yourself and tuck it into your journal.

What do you feel when you witness the woman looking back at you?

Give yourself permission to play. Adorn yourself in any manner you wish for the photograph, taken by you or another and possibly inspired by a goddess of your choosing. Frolic outdoors or in. This is grounded creative time where you can explore your Self-expression.

Write down the words that flow from Her. Give her voice. As you do, accept that everything she says is simply to be witnessed, not judged. Hold her in your heart space with compassion and love. Your image is the reflection of all women and Goddess herself.

Build an Altar to Your Inner Work

Building an altar grounds your intentions and honors the process you're participating in. Altars connect our collective memory to primal practices, which in ancient times brought us in resonance with the Divine.

Create an area where you can place candles, crystals, a goddess statue to represent Mother, incense, and any other objects special to you and which seem relevant.

You may wish to place a photograph of yourself as a child with or without mother, or just your mother or someone who represents mother to you on the altar. If you are hearing a resounding 'no' to this suggestion, journal it and re-visit later in this course-book.

Your altar may change as the months go by. You can add fresh flowers or treasures from the ocean - the womb we came from - to it or treasures from the forest or the desert. Let this spark your imagination and speak of your story.

Keep this altar alive with light and movement. Take care of it as you would your inner child. There is much symbolism and ceremony with altar creation. You are, in fact, creating a new paradigm for your Self.

Notice how the energy of the altar shifts as you do. There will be times of ebb and flow, times you are inspired by it and possibly times when you may abandon it. Just observe and journal.

You are energy. Energy must move.

Movement Practice

To help facilitate the movement of your emotions, I suggest that you decide on one physical practice that you will *enjoy*. My favorites are yoga, rebounding, gardening, and nature walks.

What is *your* best, most aligned way of creating movement in your body? Dance, surfing, tennis, bowling, golf, walking your dog, rolling around on the floor...there is no wrong way.

If you've answered, 'sex', btw, then yes! With conscious intention, sex is a sacred medium for soul evolution and a wonderful way to increase endorphins, stop mind-chatter, or move Kundalini energy.

Summary

We begin gently. Allow for your integration. These steps set the foundation for transformation. I encourage you to not skip any.

Accept the call to circle. Inscribe your intention for your Mother Wound healing on your heart and in your journal.

Begin your journal practice. Gather some or all the tools you will be using there. Make your first entries.

Take your photo and add it to your journal. Write what comes to the surface as you do.

Create an altar. If you need this to be a very private space in your home, you can create one in a box with a lid. Be careful when playing with fire in the box!!! Don't worry if it takes some time to gather everything. Just begin.

Blessings on your path, Wild, Sovereign One

My wings have been there all along, ready to help me take flight from the enveloping shadows. Sometimes the chrysalis, sometimes the butterfly, I am always exactly where I need to be to set my soul free.

SITTING WITH FEAR

Can we sit with our fear and learn to love it? Can we allow our fear to be a guide to deeper healing?

Because fear is not going anywhere—we can't erase it from our system. Right there in the innate wiring of our nervous system, is programmed our ability to work with fear.

It's a beautiful part of us that we often turn towards in hate; however, fear is a valid piece of our humanness.

The more we fight our fear, the harder it is to process and move forward from. If we don't face our fear, we run from it, or hide it and it becomes our shame.

Can we sit with our fear instead and love it?
Can we use it to remember our wholeness and to remind our self of our bravery and courage?

Abhaya is a Sanskrit word for fearlessness, which is a goal in both Buddhist and many Hindu paths. It means we do not turn away from things. Instead, we hold a stance of peacefulness and protection towards them.

The problem is not the fear. The problem becomes our avoiding of feelings that we deem as not acceptable. We are always trying to get away from ourselves when something arises that's uncomfortable. What if we loved that piece of discomfort; what if we gave that fear a beautiful embrace of reassurance.

See what happens then?
When we love something, we learn to work with it. Fear does not need to be an obstacle to our sacred healing. Fear can be an anchoring companion to it instead.

Sarah Norrad

The Alchemy of Words

We are always in transition. Expecting consistency, predictability, or a fixed identity of ourselves produces suffering. Instead, we can accept the flow of life, letting go of our tight grip on expectations and releasing the discomfort felt when we approach inevitable change. Energy cannot bear to be static. Find beauty in your continually shifting reality.

Write Your Transformation Story – Spiraling In

You are becoming the *Alchemist* – taking the base metal of wounding and turning it into the gold of self-mastery.

This is sacred work, magical work for mystics and shadow workers which in fact, we all are, when we open to possibility and spirit.

For some of us, the story is everything. For others, it is a shadow to be forgotten.

You may not entirely remember the story. It may only be surfacing now, or you may have to rely on others to help you put the pieces together. Alternatively, it may be seared with exact precision onto your consciousness. Either way, with the first step taken, you are entering new realms of relating to yourself and the world. There will be defining shifts as Universe honors your commitment.

Perhaps you recall an incident with Mother Wound that to others may seem insignificant. Or it may be the death of Mother at any stage of your life, literal or metaphorical. Wounds cannot be compared, nor can trauma. Each story holds equal value and importance.

You may be surprised at what reveals itself. This course may take you in a direction you could not have expected.

Long-buried codes within our DNA are revealed through conscious introspection.

One thing I do know from doing my own work, is that once you commit to the journey, your cells and psyche will begin their work of releasing. You will begin to dream, lucid dream, and remember in ways you may not expect. People may show up from your past. You may even be visited by the departed, angels, or spirit guides.

All of this is simply an unfolding. It does not even truly matter if you have all the facts straight. We witness ourselves to find compassion for our humanity.

This process is for you. Own it. Watch those wings unfurl!

We must own our story and know that this trauma, this tale, is a portal for finding our purpose, creativity, compassion, and unconditional love.

Wounding exposes our spirit to greater growth. There is always a nugget of Purpose embedded in the things we go through. It is for us to uncover and use for the expansion of personal and collective consciousness.

So, while it happened to us, it happened to the whole of Consciousness. We hold the collective wound. When one heals, we all heal. That is a Universal law.

"I'm re-writing my story, and it's beautiful!"

I invite you to surround yourself with anything that brings you joy while you write your story. Find comfortable, inspiring places. Drink your favorite beverage in a special cup. Perhaps take a day to go someplace you consider soulful or healing as you remember...a garden or simply spending the day in bed, cradling your inner child may call you.

Ego

You may encounter ego along the road somewhere. Ego may warn you that processing and releasing the story is dangerous. Ego may ask what right you have to go digging through things that obviously will never go away and that you must keep repeating the story, recounting the wounds, or else... who would you be without it?

Ego is NOT a self-aware mechanism.

Ego fears death because it cannot imagine life after death – and so it clings. It will try to protect you by convincing you that forgiveness and healing are impossible. You see, to the ego, *transformation means certain death*. Spiritual wisdom acknowledges that life and death are inseparable. If we live, we die; if we die, we live. These cycles are very eminent in our lives. We go through many deaths and re-births during one lifetime. The false safety that ego provides in this situation is one that keeps us in wound mode if we can't discern the bullshit from the buckwheat.

Ego is an essential part of human life. It keeps us alive in the real world with its freeze, flight, or fight reflex. But when it comes to transformation, it is miserably lost in its own fight for survival.

When ego and inner critics arrive, treat them with compassion but hold strong boundaries.

After this module, your story may become background information - research material for your soul growth. It will not be something the wound feeds on but learns from. The story is to be honored, valued for its lessons, bathed in light, kept in perspective, and released so the wound can close.

Our wounds are veils or filters through which we experience our world. They are not who we are. They are an experience we can move through.

'Who am I without this veil, this story?'

It may come as a surprise that beyond this veil we are whole. Be curious about yourself, the soul who is evolving through many lifetimes, many veils.

The Challenge

Journal your story. You may also paint it, dance it, sing it, play it, or any combination of these modalities.

You may not be able to put it down on paper, YET. Begin where you can.

When you write your story, you are supporting millions of women whose stories have never been heard and who have been silenced forever.

Your Story is Her story.

What is your Mother Wound as you conceptualize it in this moment?

Tips for Writing

First person or third person account? You choose. Third person may feel safer at first for some.

The masterpiece is YOU, not the story. Not a writer? No worries. Just write your heart.

Don't agonize over details or flow. Let it come as it wants.

The story may be sparse at first, or full of detail. The goal is to open the container. It is enough.

Begin...

To create a consciousness shift around our story, to make a quantum leap from trauma bond, co-dependence with trauma, stepping out of the triangle of disempowerment between the Perpetrator, the Victim, and the Rescuer, we write two versions.

Story One is written from the level and archetype of the Serpent – our belly to the ground, very sensory, our perspective is limited, it is survival, freeze, fight, or flight response.

This is the story that the mind and ego are trapped in and which forms emotions to feed the pain.

It looks for a savior or rescuer, which can manifest in the form of a therapist, a lover, or the illusion that one day the perpetrator will be conscious of how they hurt us, apologize, take responsibility. Or it may arrive in the form of an addiction or any number of self-destructive habits, such as believing our own self-deprecating thoughts.

You are in the element of Earth, in the direction of South.

One could begin with:

1. My story is one of narcissistic abuse, abandonment, betrayal, etc.
2. The people or person who were part of my present sadness/pain/internalized trauma are ____.
3. When I was ____ old, my mother... (Tell the story.)
4. This is not what should have happened, I should have been able to experience ___. (Insert what you wish life had been at that time.)
5. I am so angry/sad/hurt/unable to move on. (Name all the ways your human is stuck.)

Or you may imagine another way to begin the story. Listen to intuition.

You can pinpoint one incident or several that were key, and which play a major role in your memories, or you can pick one thing from your mother, father, and grandmother that you find particularly painful or unforgivable, and which shaped your existence.

You're not trying to figure anything out here or find resolution. It's simply a story of 'this should not have happened' that is what the mind keeps holding on to. Later this story will be something that can no longer trigger you into lingering with the PTSD of trauma.

Then we move on to the second story, which has a very different purpose.

At the end of the second story, ideally, the serpent sheds her skin all at once as it ceases to identify with herself as the victim. She simply leaves the story behind and the mind/ego's attachment to it. Then, when sadness arises over something that happened, one can love that sadness and have compassion for it instead of joining it on an epic journey of cellular pain.

Story one is the same story one has lived for many lifetimes, and though one may have learned many lessons over each lifetime, there is a central theme that is repeated. This is our 3D experience.

We can't blame anyone for it. We take responsibility for our soul's path and the lesson it chose. We also do not blame ourselves for anything. 3D life is non-sensical to our human perception of logic, but it remains our soul's path to learn through adversity and polarity.

Notice that fairy tales follow this pattern. There is a poor helpless person, the big bad wolf, and the rescuer. Nothing empowering here.

I personally feel that in 4D/5D we transcend having to learn from these archetypes over and over again.

Story two is the beginning of our 4D/5D experience.

When I realized my pain came from wanting to be liked, I started to love myself.

When I realized my pain came from wanting to be acknowledged, I began to see the woman I really was.

When I realized my pain came from hoping to be special, I set out to explore the depths of my normality.

When I realized my pain came from wanting to be held, I let myself feel the sensations of my body.

When I realized my pain came from craving to belong, I took the first steps to nourish my authentic self.

When I realized my pain originated from the actions of others, I began to accept responsibility for my own story.

When I realized my pain came from chasing those who didn't want me, I set myself free.

Tanya Markul, The She Book

Mother Wound is the portal for finding your purpose, creativity, compassion, and love for others. The story is not the real story. The real story is your unfolding.

Story Two

(Choose to begin writing story two now, near the middle, or at the end of this book journey.)

In story two, you are the heroine of your own story. You take responsibility for your own experience. The mind and ego are not fighting with what wasn't fair or who is to blame. One recognizes their story as the absolute perfect occurrence for soul evolution and alchemy.

You are in the element of West. Jaguar. The Luminous Warrior.

You no longer wear your story medicine as armour to protect yourself.

Here are some elements of Story Two. You can answer in one sentence or a volume. Speak what needs speaking.

1. Where are your ancestors from? Connect with your culture, the wombs you came from, etc.) –
   I was born in ____, to ____.
2. My medicine is ____. (Teaching others through your experience, creativity you have embarked on that facilitates healing for yourself and others – anything you have to offer because of your transformation.)
3. But it wasn't always this way... There was a time when...

> *In my personal story I said "I was completely unaware of my place in life. I was an orphan, sexually abused, dissociated" – and on it went. This is a bit of retelling of what happened, but as interesting information, looking back,* **this is the valley you rose from**.

4. My story tells...

> *Example: My story tells the evolution of my soul. It is the path I chose to help me hone the strong medicine I have for the world. I feel so much love and compassion for the courage I have had to live my many lifetimes. Now I know that in order to become the teacher I have had to be the student and embrace my story as one of the illuminated warriors.*

You can word this in any way you wish or expand on this further.

5. I feel called to share my medicine in a humble and powerful way because I understand the pain of many souls and am able to hold them in unconditional love. I am empowered on my chosen path. I understand that my wounding did not happen to me but through me. (...or something like this. The last sentence shows the transcendence from victim to heroine of your own story.)

Moving Forward - Journal This

1. Who will you be without this wound?
2. Can you imagine a life where it no longer influences your mood, emotions, physical body, or spiritual awareness? Bring these questions and any insights to your journal.
3. Are you thinking of sharing your story?
4. If yes, is this the first time you will have shared it?
5. Who will you share it with?
6. How does it feel to give the story wings?
7. Are you sharing it differently than you did or would have before?

Self-Care

As with any cleansing process, your story may trigger detox symptoms. You are beginning to shed your old skin.

Drink plenty of water (moving through), rest (you may be more tired than usual), allow the tears (honoring emotions), and nourish your body with live, vibrant food.

Summary

Write Your Story: Spiraling In – Story One and Two

Nurture Your Writing Space – You, your story and your process deserve an intentionally supportive atmosphere

The Role of Ego & Tips for Writing

Who Will You Be Without this Wound?

Journal Prompts

Self-Care

"He Who Knows Others is Wise.
He Who Knows Himself is Enlightened."

Lao Tzu

"To Know Thyself is the Beginning of Wisdom"

Socrates

Know Yourself

*I am safe to be in my fullness and take up all the space I
need in the world. I am safe to pursue the path I
envisioned, desired, and trained for before my
incarnation. The whole of the Universe, my guides, and
my ancestors support me on my journey.
I embody my purpose.*

Numerology and **Astrology** are powerful tools which can guide us on the journey of Self-Discovery.

The natural world offers us many signs and systems which can be viewed as portals to our Inner World.

As we are made of the stars and are ambassadors from other planetary systems to this world, we can take cues from the very mystery of which we are made.

The more we understand the magic of our own incarnation, what planets, moons and energies work with our personality and soul-designed destiny, the more we can unfold into our sacred journey. Unfolding in this way, we can find the grace, self-forgiveness and empathy needed to actualize and take full space in our humanity and spirituality.

Further to this, we can understand the Mother Archetype and its role in our life. We can answer the unanswerable questions of our past and present. There is a great liberation in understanding Self, a great ownership of our patterns and expectations.

We do not seek to change ourselves, but to befriend and love Self. From this place, we can entertain new visions of growth.

In my 'Soul Mission' Workbook, available through my website, I outline how to map our soul's desire for this particular incarnation.

If you are working with an astrologer, make sure you find what your North Node, South Node, Moon and Chiron information and placements are.

North Node: The Unknown - Our Soul's Fulfillment, where we lift ourselves to our highest vibration, our Higher Self. It indicates our life purpose in this life. It is where we step into the unknown, being guided by the light of awareness.

South Node: The Known - Issues to complete, closure of old identities. Shows where we may get stuck in old habits that are familiar and comfortable, that were helpful in the past but no longer serve us, baggage from past and present life.

Moon: Mother Aspect. How the moon's placement in our chart influences our emotions and childhood memories. *The Mother embodies love, fertility, nourishment, responsibility, patience, power, self-care. She invites you to master giving and receiving love.*

Chiron: Placement shows our childhood wounds and the healing that can come of it.

If you are casting your own chart online, use a reliable astro-site. This is a great place to begin until you find an astrologer whose work and philosophies resonate with you.

1. Bring to your journal any newly discovered aspects of Self through astrology. Be curious about what makes you unique.
2. There will never be another human being with your unique astrological influences. This means that no one else on the planet can bring to it what you do. You are mysteriously made, and the planets reveal all.

Major Life Transits

Another important aspect of knowing ourselves is found through the work of Barbara Hand Clow. She outlines four Major Astrological Life Transits that offer incredible clarity on our evolving consciousness while in human form. They are hosted by Saturn, Chiron, and Uranus.

In the past, shamanic societies recognized and celebrated rites of passage within the tribe. We have done away with most rituals initiating us into different stages of life, and have lost the sacredness that comes with recognizing the varied phases a human can pass through.

Concurrently, we have lost touch with, never known, or forgotten the knowledge of key astrological transits through the natal chart, which have a profound effect on our rise in consciousness.

Barbara Hand Clow defines what these transits are, how they affect us, and how we can navigate them for our human and spiritual evolution.

To know which stage one is at or approaching allows for a mindful transit which can be the difference between life and death, literally or metaphorically. You can discover more in my workbook, but here are the main points:

1. **Birth to age 30** - Forming the I AM. The Physical Plane. First Saturn Return. Saturn asks - life or death? What shall we do with our lives, who shall we mature into? The Maiden.

2. **Age 30 to 42** - Perfecting the Emotional Plane. Mid-Life Crisis. Kundalini Rising. Integrating our Polar Opposite. Stepping into Power. Uranus Opposition. The Mother.

3. **Age 42 to 50** - Development of the Mind. Balance. Spiritual Awakening at 50. We become Whole. Chiron Return.

4. **Age 58 to 60** - Stepping into Wisdom. Another Chance to Unfold into Purpose. Eros/Death theme re-visited. Second Saturn Return. The Crone.

For other important transits, more detail on each life period, I recommend 'Astrology and the Rising of Kundalini' by Barbara Hand Clow

Charting Your Course

There are many roads that one can take, many ways to find creative expression of Self, and none of those roads are wrong. All roads taken are some forms of self-discovery.

We meet ourselves time and time again in a thousand guises on the paths of life

Carl Jung

According to numerology, Pythagorean mysticism/philosophy, and sacred geometry, we are inherently designed to embody certain desires, traits, and journeys.

In this way, Universe discovers itself and creates through our experiences. In this way, we discover the Universe within Self.

Knowing our Life Path, Soul Urge, and Destiny Numbers and their meanings can help illuminate the dark corners of why we're here. You can find online calculators for these, or decipher it on your own, then look up the meanings.

What lies before us and what lies behind us are small matters compared to what lies within us. And when we bring what lies within out into the world, miracles happen.

Henry David Thoreau

I recommend *The Life You Were Born to Live* by Dan Millman for a more in-depth study of your life-path number as well as the numerology for your family and friends. Otherwise, work with a numerologist like myself, or consult with online interpretations/numerology books.

Find Your Birth Number by Your Own Calculation

Your Birthdate: Month/Day/Year
example: 11/04/1972

Reduce the month, day, and year down to a single digit by adding them.
example: 1+1+4+1+9+7+2= 25=7

Life path #7

By this calculation, your Life Path Map to explore in D. Millman's book would be 25/7 or use any numerology apps to guide your way.

*An excellent North Node book to explore is *Astrology for the Soul* by Jan Spiller.

GETTING TO KNOW MOTHER

What is your Mother's Birth date, tarot influence, sun sign and life path number?

Just as knowing ourselves leads to true embodiment, knowing the woman whose womb birthed us can lead to greater self-understanding (where you came from), self-love (what happened has many roots), and a dissolution of anger, grudges, blame.

It can lead to compassionate dialogue, even forgiveness.

At the least, it will shed light onto the path before you. At most, it will free you.

Witness Mother's journey.

Enter into this gently. Our mind wants to cling to the pain, because, as we discussed before, the ego resists transformation. But with an intentional and compassionate exploration, we can come to seeing Mother with more clarity.

CHARTING A NEW COURSE

- *What have you discovered about yourself through your birth chart that helps you understand your choices, thoughts, and inclinations towards life? Perhaps you have had a birth chart reading previously. Do you have new insights through another look?*

- *Does this inspire you to have more compassion for yourself and to see your journey with more introspection? How?*

- *How does knowing Mother's life path number allow for better understanding of her as a woman on her own journey, and how does it compare to yours? Do her choices make more sense now?*

- *Intuit into your body and recognize how it felt to read about her life path number influences. What came up? Understanding or judgement? (Do not judge the reaction, simply observe)*

- *Delve deeper into the numbers, astrology. Perhaps create a colorful art board depicting your Self as your sun sign, numbers, planet placements. Include a poem or thought you have written to yourself.*

- *Do you wish to include Mother and her influences in this art project, or do you wish to journey alone? Can you sense where you are headed? Let your intuition guide who this space is for.*

Summary

Important Aspects of Your Birth Chart

What Astro Transit Are You Living Now? Can You Recall Major Events That Happened at the Different Stages? Where Are You Headed? Journal Insights

The Life You Were Born to Live - Life Path Numbers - What are the Numbers Which Influence Your Current Incarnation?

Discovering Mother's Life Path Number. Observing Reactions and Shifts in Expectations

Putting It All Together/Charting a New Course - A New Understanding of Self in Relation to Mother's Self. Standing in Your Authentic Journey. Giving Space to Hers.

The Mother Archetype

Empowered. I am not a victim of circumstance. I claim my sovereignty and agency. I claim choice and my voice. I take personal responsibility for the choices I make.

"The birth mother is always the death mother and vise-versa."

Clarissa Pinkola Estés

Carl Jung considered the Mother archetype most important of all because it seemed to encompass all other archetypes.

Archetype: universal thought-forms or mental images that influence an individual's feelings and actions

We become familiar with archetypes very early on, through fairy tales, myths, or religions, through dreams and cultural stories. Contained within the collective unconscious, archetypes help us make sense of our outer world, the mysteries of the cosmos and nature - which, paradoxically, helps us to make sense of our inner world. To actualize Self and our personal purpose on earth, we must ironically venture beyond Self and delve into Collective Wisdom. Archetypes help us to understand the human consciousness and psyche.

"Mother' is a complex and deeply mystical thought-form."

Carl Jung

We are born of the womb, a dark, primordial space within which all of creation manifests. It is literal and metaphorical. It is the ocean, from where all life evolved. It is the Void, from which the Universe unfolded. It is comforting, warm, nourishing, safe, and dark.

It is in darkness that we are formed and through darkness that we *transform*. It is our mother's womb. We are, as a species, hard-wired for Mother.

Through religion, we learn of the saintly mother. The good mother. The impossibly perfect mother. Through fairy tales, we meet the dark mother, the stepmother, the incapable mother, and sometimes the good mother...but she always seems to die early on leaving us to learn the harsh realities of life.

Sometimes the fairy-godmother steps into her role. Other times, we are rescued from the bad mother by a masculine figure.

As a collective consciousness, we have great expectations of Mother as well as the Divine Masculine, which forms a basis of co-dependence.

The truth is, Mother often does not live up to our expectations. We may mistake our mother for the archetypal ideal. She is a reflection of the Great Mother, and to understand her we need to understand the Great Mother and *her* wound.

The Mystery

Goddess Takes Many Forms.

She is manifested in The Great Mother (Creatress), in Gaia (Mother Nature), in Divine Feminine energy and expression (present in all genders) and is birthed from the Spirit realm to the physical world via WOMAN who becomes Mother and is likewise, DAUGHTER.

The mystery of the Triple Goddess - Maiden, Mother, Crone - is reflected in the phases of the moon and the cycles of Birth, Life, Death, and Re-birth.

Woman is the mystery physically representing the Great
Mother, the Divine Feminine, and the Triple Goddess.

She, like nature, can create, sustain, *and* destroy.
Sometimes she is the gentle rain, sometimes the monsoon.
Sometimes the quiet river and other times the tsunami.
Sometimes sunshine, sometimes thunder. She is ever
evolving, sometimes the earthquake.

*She gives us our footing and then requires us to find our
own. When we see Mother as a mirror for nature, and
nature as a mirror for mother, we understand that
Mother is not always safe mother.*

Safe mother would do it all for us, keep us from spreading
our wings. Our life would be very one-dimensional, and we
would never understand how to interpret danger living
with the *too-safe* mother. We would believe every stranger
that came along because safe mother does not teach us to
trust our intuition.

**Many daughters have said that they felt their
whole life was about surviving Mother.**

And should we dig deeper still, the root of the struggle is
with the Great Mother, Goddess, Nature herself, because
within our centuries old survival instinct, we have felt
abandoned by Goddess and by our mother planet through
many natural disasters, famines and shifts in Her body.

Sadly, the Great Mother also carries the collective wound
of human impact upon her soil and her oceans. Every act of
environmental genocide carried out against the Great
Mother is embodied by Woman. Every act of violence
against women since the beginning of time is carried
within the cell memory and DNA of Woman. Our suffering
and healing are intertwined.

**Healing Mother wound is deeply personal yet gives
rise to a stronger community worldwide.**

The Great Mother, the Divine Feminine and Woman, long in conflict with the Shadow side of the Masculine (Patriarchy), has had to withdraw from her inherent nature to survive.

She has -

Rejected her instincts and intuition
She has hidden and denied her wisdom
She has abandoned herself and her dreams
She may not fit the role of Mother and Divine Feminine as outlined by society
She has not held her Self or been able to nurture her vulnerable Inner Child
She has given in to her own rage at her inability to rise sovereign
She has been deemed hysterical, unstable, untrustworthy, crazy, too emotional, too much, too little
She has endured medical interference with her cycles, birthing process, unnecessary surgeries, hormonal disruptors; aimed at keeping her wild nature at bay
She has been told to mind her mouth
She has been raped, burned, drowned
Her lakes, rivers, oceans, forests and farmlands have been systematically destroyed
She has directed her unhappiness and lack of purpose at her mirror image, her daughter
Nature, The Divine Feminine and Woman have become 'resources' to be exploited

Such denial of Self builds grief and rage. Rage creates wildfires and tsunamis. Rage creates mothers who cannot support the life they gave birth to. Grief consumes everything in its path.

At some point along the way, often at too young an age, we begin to absorb our mothers' pain. We take it on as our own. We don't trust our intuition. We doubt our wisdom. We attract partners who mirror our lack of self-love. We don't trust our emotions. The cycle continues.

Empowerment lies in the awareness that our unhappiness is not the responsibility of our mother. Unhappiness may stem from our relationship with mother, but it is our own responsibility. Re-framed, we can own our rising, free from the tether to which we had enslaved ourselves.

What is Mother? The Road to Restoration

Mother is all things, just as the Great Mother is all things.

She is the kind, nurturing woman, the white witch, the kind, wise queen, the innocent princess. She is Luna, lighting our path.

She is the hag, the dark witch, the angry, jealous queen, the destructive force of nature. She is Kali, breathing fire.

As soon as we see Mother in all her versions, we can find compassion for the woman who, through her incarnation as the Divine Feminine, mirrors the complexity of the Goddess.

As soon as we give up the fantasy of the 'good mother,' we can embrace the light and shadow within *ourselves* and further, our own mother.

The destruction of Woman as healer, creatress, sorceress, wise woman, alchemist, and birther of consciousness has led to detachment from Self and purpose.

This is ours to re-birth and resurrect within us through healing mother wound.

The Invitation

The invitation is to witness your mother
as these archetypes:

Goddess
Wise Woman
Healer
Creatress

When you witness someone, you are giving space for their joy, their pain, their successes, their failures, their light, and their dark. You are honoring their Beingness in the same way you wish to be honored.

1.   In meditation or reflection, allow an image of the archetypal 'Woman' to come to mind. See her in the way she has been unseen and unheard through millennia. There is a natural compassion for Woman because she is you and you are her. To support her is to support yourself. The time is now, on the planet, for women to stand together and reclaim their magic.

2.   Imagine now your mother merging with Woman, her face is the face of all women. She is the embodiment of all the healing that must occur within the Mother archetype. Witness your mother.

     If you can envision it, look into her eyes. See the woman, the divine feminine, the great mother, the goddess.

3.   As you do this, you are also peering into your own consciousness, your humanity. See yourself as the divine feminine, the great mother, goddess.

A Shamanic Ritual

MOTHER AS AVATAR FOR WOMAN

In the spirit of sisterhood, within the Meditation realm, invite Archetypal Woman/Your Mother, to a virtual healing circle.

This embodiment exercise is meant to take place within the spirit realm, **but** if your heart is calling for a physical healing circle, then by all means, invite your mother to join you.

Gather: Meditation/circle dance music, drum, tambourine, rattle or any instrument of your choice, journal. A spot near your altar.

1. Light the candles on your altar, get comfortable, let yourself fall into the music you have chosen.

2. Close your eyes and silently imagine witnessing each other through your Third Eye. Imagine the journey of Woman through time, all she has endured and survived. Extend blessings to her, thanking her for her strength and fortitude, for her tears and her wisdom.

3. Imagine that you are making an offering to Woman. A gift of a shell, or a raven feather; anything that comes to mind. Or you can place something on your altar as an actual gift.

4. Accept any gift she may have for you. Acknowledge that she is another you and you are another her.

5. Now as the two of you join hands for a sacred circle dance, other women begin to appear, women from many lifetimes, your ancestry, and all tribes. You begin to dance together and play your instruments. You offer

laughter and support. Your Mother melts into the many women around the circle. She, and you, are the women who are beginning to remember.

Wise One, Healer, Lover, Mother, Sister, Daughter, Creatress, Aunt, Inner Child, Witch, Luna, Kali, Divine Feminine, Goddess. This is the awakening.

6. Dance for as long as you wish, connecting through your imagination to all the women you have invited to your circle. Make note of and journal in your own timing –

Who comes?
Who sits on the side, afraid to participate?
Who succumbs to tears?
Who softens?
What gifts are shared?
Who hardens?
Who leaves?

End your dance by passing an imaginary or real squeeze of the hand beginning with you and ending with you. Each squeeze is accompanied by the mantra:

"I witness you as you are. I love you as you are.'

Know that as you say these words you are also saying them to yourself.

Release Woman/Your Mother and all the women in the circle into the spirit realm.

7. Finish the meditation in Child's Pose if able. This is a perfect pose for surrendering to the journey you are on. It is a place of no-thought, it elongates the spine moving spinal fluid or kundalini energy from the base to your brain, stretches the hips where we hold emotions and trauma, it is resting in what is.

Witnessing Mother in Her Many Forms

(an excerpt from my Wise Woman Mystery School)

MOTHER IS HOME

To tap into Mother Archetype is to find our way back home, to before our incarnation, to the place where our soul came from (our spiritual self), and it is also honoring our human self.

There are times when we feel lost, ungrounded, yearning for something undefined. What we search for is wholeness.

Through daily life, we scatter bits of ourselves in many different directions. Mother archetype can help us bring those pieces back together.

1. Choose a sunny day and find a spot in nature that feels supportive and safe.

2. Bring a blanket, some of your favorite comfort food, a flask of tea or coffee, your journal, and some magical items from your altar, plus a gift for Earth Mother.

3. Take a few moments to settle, notice the beauty around you, in gratitude for your surroundings and being able to take this time to yourself.

4. Lie down on the earth. Feel her beneath you, supporting and loving you. Sink you bones deeply, imagine growing roots.

5. Now visualize the pieces you have lost to worry, anger, fear, circumstance.

6. Imagine a compassionate, loving, mother figure helping you gather these pieces and handing them to you. Imagine her placing her hands over your heart as you breathe yourself back together. Take your time in this magical place.

7. Feel the generosity and wholeness she provides. Allow yourself to receive and integrate. Stay here for a while.

8. Open your eyes when you feel complete.

9. Look around you. Does the world look different? How do you feel? Indulge in your picnic. When leaving, place your gift somewhere inconspicuous for Earth Mother.

An Abundance/Reciprocity Meditation

Open your arms wide, pull your spine up straight, and breathe in deeply.

Take a moment to 'feel' your hands, become aware of them as part of you.

Visualize your heart opening wide. Take a moment. Feel it.

Receive the energy of abundance through your left palm. Allow it to travel up your arm to your heart.

Take a moment for your heart to fill with gratitude. Feel the abundance.

Continue the flow down your right arm, to your right palm.

Bring your hands together at heart center, transferring the energy back to your left palm.

Repeat as many times as you wish.

Mid Lesson Summary

Which aspects of Mother/Goddess/Healer/Wise Woman do you feel your mother was able to embody with grace and empowerment or with the greatest challenge?

Which do you feel you are able to embody and how do you view your shared journey to that embodiment?

Are there similarities or are your paths divergent?

FINDING A GIFT FOR MOTHER

Which Mother would you like to share a gift with? Choose between Mother Nature, your mother, a mother figure. A gift for yourself closes the circle as you validate your role in representing the Great Mother.

Have fun with the gift. The suggestion is a crystal, pebble, or feather, but could be planting a tree, creating a craft from natural elements, or writing a song.

Continue with your movement practice. Are you seeing a flow of energy that wasn't there before as a result of your practice?

Self-Embodiment is a woman's pilgrimage home.

Mother Archetype and Patriarchy

"Civilized Man says: I am Self, I am Master, all the rest is other - outside, below, underneath, subservient. I own, I use, I explore, I exploit, I control. What I do is what matters. What I want is what matter is for. I am that I am, and the rest is women & wilderness, to be used as I see fit."

Ursula K. Le Guin

"No male successfully measures up to patriarchal standards without engaging in an ongoing practice of self-betrayal."

Bell Hooks

In sharing these two quotes, I suggest that it is the shadow side of the Divine Masculine which has long participated in destroying the sovereignty and well-being of Woman, Gaia, and reverence for The Great Mother, as embodied by the Mother Archetype.

In order for a person identifying as male (or equally a person identifying as female) to engage with patriarchal energy, they must first betray their beginnings as an incarnated impulse of Love.

Since the beginning of time, Woman has created magic, healing, held space and honed her intuition using what Great Mother offered naturally - sticks, stones, and the alchemy of her love.

Her wisdom driven underground through the distortion and dissonance of Patriarchy. She now seeks new ground, rising, re-birthing, awakening.

Healing Mother Wound births new paradigms and restructures our DNA and the DNA of Consciousness.

It challenges patriarchy at its core. Yes, we, as individuals can create massive shifts in the fabric of societal evolution by addressing how patriarchy has affected our Mother-line.

THE ROLE OF PATRIARCHY WITHIN MOTHER ARCHETYPE

Sociologist Sylvia Walby describes **Patriarchy** as "a system of social structures and practices in which men dominate, oppress, and exploit women".

Through many social systems and institutions developed over time - religious, educational, etc., both men and women have embodied Patriarchy.

The Mother Archetype, which shape-shifts according to the energy of the Age we are in, (currently shifting from Piscean to Age of Aquarius), is realizing an awareness that the domination of women and the planet is a system which can be re-created into a healthy one.

The Piscean Age: Chakra - Solar Plexus - Power, Ego, Control, Hierarchy

Age of Aquarius: Chakra - Heart - Love, Service, Harmony, Freedom, Equality

There were many positive aspects of the Piscean Age such as artistry, spirituality, (Age of Jesus - so much to do with the element of water), advancement in technology, etc., but most of it was led and recorded through *his-story*.

As the Age of Aquarius began its initial influence a few centuries ago, it sought a balancing of the predominantly masculine energy on the planet, and we began to see the rise of gentler, more inclusive movements.

Aspects of the Masculine:
Expressive, Decisive, Concrete, Assertive

Aspects of the Feminine:
Intuitive, Abstract, Tranquil, Receptive

In balance, they evolve into a society evolving to heart-based philosophies.

The Divine Feminine, The Great Mother, Gaia, Woman, rises as she is called to the service of humanity.

The work of healing Mother Wound is the work of many hearts joined in ushering in the Age of Aquarius.

We heal to live through the heart, so the whole of society can live through the heart.

* Patriarchy can be embodied by a person of any gender. It does not only evolve through the visually masculine, because the Masculine, just as the Feminine, is an integral part of all Beings. To dismantle patriarchy, we must be willing to look at where it lives within ourselves and be willing to dismantle the shadows of dominance and subjugation.

Dreaming A New Age
Exploring How Patriarchy Influenced Your Story

The Immature Masculine, disconnected from his emotions, vulnerability, ability to express his emotions, unsupported in his emotional development by Mother, trained into manhood by a misogynistic society and Father, lashes out at all that represents the Feminine, Intuition, and what he deems as the chaos of female emotions.

Awed by the Feminine's ability to birth all of humanity and bring Spirit into human form by the magic of her blood and womb, Father seeks to engage with blood alchemy, but he can only do so through shedding it in war and aggression. He draws his false power through violence, oppression, and domination. Disconnected from the responsibility of his actions, he is unrepentant and unaware of his privilege.

In *his* primary relationship with Mother, he remains an infant who at once seeks the comfort of what She represents (this includes all of nature, the planet, resources) and at the same time holds great disrespect for her gifts, expressing his disrespect through his relationships with partners, children, and his environment.

Men who live through the heart create the template for men who through their conditioning, cannot access their vulnerability and compassion.

Women who have the support of their partners to raise vulnerable, compassionate sons, create a new heart template for the Aquarian Man.

The Aquarian Man can participate in supporting the Divine Feminine in Her role as Mother/Daughter. The Mother Archetype evolves toward 5th Dimension Consciousness.

Your Mother Line, seeped for centuries in the predominant philosophy of the Piscean Age, has sometimes willingly or unwillingly participated in misogyny and patriarchy and the fall-out of that on your own story.

"As Burning Women, our maternal lines probably go back through many, many women who shut down to their fire, were burned by others, and whose fires burned them, their families and their marriages alive. We are the descendants of grandmothers and mothers who each handled the fire in their own way, trying to survive"

Burning Woman – Lucy H. Pierce

EXPLORING PATRIARCHY WITHIN YOUR MOTHER-LINE

1. Where in your story do you see influences of patriarchy and misogyny, and did it create a disconnect within the mother/daughter relationship directly or indirectly?

2. Can you see how your mother and/or grandmother took on the philosophy and actions of patriarchy within your family, perhaps not embodying the Feminine but subjugating to the will of the Immature Masculine in their actions and thought patterns? How did this affect how they mothered you?

3. Do you think they were aware of this influence on their life or even had the clarity to think this through or were they acting in survival mode as women within a patriarchal society?

4. As women who were most likely not seen or heard, did they pass on their frustration and anger to the next generation? How so within your own story?

5. Can you give an example(s) how you may have continued this cycle or ways you did not?

6. What new processes can you implement within your own life and that of your family which support the Divine Feminine and the Mother Archetype in healing the wounds of the collective mother wound?

7. What wisdom can you pass on to your children or your younger, present, or future Self that will guide your healing and actions?

8. How has your mother's fire been doused by patriarchy? Give any examples you can think of.

Can you stand in compassion for this woman stripped of her power and her fire?

9. What can you offer her in words to show her that you witness her inability to rise about those circumstances and her choices within those circumstances?

10. Write a message or letter to express your emotions about this, where the pain lies.

11. What are some ways you can claim back your own power which may have been taken away through Patriarchy?

*When we show understanding and compassion
for the women before us who embodied patriarchy
and misogyny, we are not condoning their choices or
actions, but are standing with all women who lived
with their power unexpressed in positive ways.
We own our pain and our disappointment, while
simultaneously giving voice to it as we write,
speak, paint, or dance it. When we claim our
freedom of patriarchal thought or action, we claim
it for all women.*

Summary

Explore Patriarchy within Self, your immediate family, and your mother-line.

Answer any or all questions which apply to your own situation/story.

Add an item to your altar which represents the Mature Masculine to support the goddess/mother image you have there.

Engage with the Masculine in a conversation about the role of Patriarchy in his relationship with his mother/the feminine. (Can be a partner or friend)

We can use our difficulties and problems
to awaken our hearts.

Pema Chödrön

Chakra Alignments

FROM THE VEDIC TRADITION

The first goddess whose magic and influence we become
intimate with is the woman whose womb we chose.

Mother becomes the source, physically, emotionally,
spritually. Our relationship with the Goddess is woven
alongide our relationship with Mother

Base and 10ᵗʰ Chakras

I AM

The base chakra resonates deeply with the mantra *I Am*.

It is an energetic place of calm and grounding.

This is the Chakra most affected by a lack of safety and place within the mother/child relationship.

BASE CHAKRA CORRESPONDENCES

Sanskrit name: Muladhara, or *root support*

Element: Earth
Location: Base of spine, tailbone, between anus and genitals
Color: Red
Deals with: Security, Survival Instinct, Fear and Abundance, Tribe, Embodiment

In alignment, Self can focus on expansion, embodiment, manifesting a desired earth experience, and a connection the Great Mother - with nature and her cycles.

Out of alignment, life is viewed through a lens of fear, insecurity and is in a basic fight for survival. Stress becomes a common cause of illness. One may not trust society or authority in general, and most poignantly, not trust Self. Inability to trust nature, focus on material possessions.

Purpose: A link for the Spiritual Being to the material/physical world. Serves as the basis for the evolution of the personality and self-expression.

Symbol: Four petaled lotus
Essential Oils: Cedar, Myrrh, Clove, Marjoram
Gemstones: Garnet, Ruby, Bloodstone, Smoky Quartz,
Black Tourmaline, Black Onyx plus other black, dark, or
reddish stones
Planets and Zodiac: Mars, Scorpio, Capricorn, Saturn,
Aries, Taurus
Glands: Adrenals
Body Parts: Bones, teeth, prostate, limbs, nails, intestines

While in utero, we absorb our mother's emotions and her
addictions (physical and emotional). We are already
borrowing from our mother's experience and adopting it
into our own psychology. We learn by example and mirror
the one whose heartbeat has been our sole companion for
the first nine months of life.

Once out into the physical world, as ego begins the work of
evolving the personality, we encounter Mother's sense of
worthiness (or lack of) as well as her ego. The infant does
not recognize that they are separate from Mother. We
begin the dance of pleasing her while continuing to find
our own ground. Childhood never seems to end when in
relationship with mother. Do you notice that her presence,
her memory, or her words can quickly rip away a carefully
built footing? This is where the work lies - stone by stone,
taking down the walls of co-dependence.

Base Chakra strength is the foundation upon which we
build our whole physical existence. It rebuilds our
foundation with tools which remind us of our sovereignty
and reason for being.

COMMON SYMPTOMS OF BASE CHAKRA MISALIGNMENT

Symptoms may ebb and flow throughout life, decreasing or
increasing with circumstances or the ability to work on
these shadows, or there may be one predominant
symptom. You may recognize some which have been

resolved and others which show up with consistency. Awareness is key as some symptoms shape shift into illness, or we keep running into others who mirror the symptoms to us when we can't see them within ourselves.

- Lack of self-trust, trusting others, trusting life itself
- Inability to build and maintain healthy boundaries
- Choosing un-supportive relationships or situations
- Lack of self-love, self-appreciation
- Difficulty aligning heart and throat chakras
- Resistance to forgiveness and letting go of resentments
- Feeling unsupported by the Universe
- Fear is a common motivating factor as opposed to faith
- Lack of self-confidence
- Perpetuating the cycle we learned during childhood

When a child finds home, safety, and love in relationship with her mother, a mother confident in her role as nurturer for the life she has birthed, the child can build their own sense of self and confidence upon this foundation. A child who cannot find that healthy attachment, develops unhealthy attachments wherever she may find them. The wounded mother may even desire or try her best to provide healthy attachment but may not have the emotional tools or be grounded enough herself to be that positive influence.

STRATEGIES FOR GROUNDING

1. Eat grounding foods – root vegetables, meat, beans, grains.

2. Walk barefoot.

3. Use the color red in clothing and home surroundings.

4. Use crystals and essential oils on the body, in meditation or healing rituals.

5. Practice rituals which have meaning to you. One is a tea ritual with mindful attention to details such as cups used, time taken, aroma and reverent pouring. Ritual making is a calming, centering activity practiced within many cultures and religions because of its ability to align the base chakra with the intention of the activity.

6. Connect with nature regularly - Great Mother.

7. Drink plenty of good water.

8. Swim or lie in moving bodies of water, or alternatively in the bath or shower. Walk in the rain. The negative ions emitted during a rainstorm clear negativity.

9. Meditate. Allow for stillness and silence.

10. Follow the cycles of the moon, planets, and seasons.

11. Journal. The practice of writing or recording events, thoughts and emotions connects spirit with the physical realm.

12. Lie naked on the earth.

13. Choose I Am statements as daily affirmations for full embodiment.

10TH CHAKRA GROUNDING MEDITATION

Where is the 10th chakra?

There are three schools of thought as to where it is; one is 1.5 feet below your feet/earth, another locates it at 3 feet below, and yet another has it above the crown between the 9th and 11th chakra.

My witch/pagan/druid tradition recognizes it as anywhere between 1.5 and 3 feet below the earth. We'll be working with that premise and intention here.

A quickie recap of the chakras:
Chakras 1 through 7 reside within the body

Outside the body and directly above the crown chakra are:
Number 8 - Connection to the Divine
Number 9 - The Seat of the Soul
Number 11 - Mind over Matter
Number 12 - Universal Unity

Our chakras connect us with the Seat of Creation. Imagine an energetic cord grounding us to Mother Earth all the way through our lower body and up through the crown, to the ether, to the stars and outer space. Our One-ness is manifested through this system, and it's how we're all energetically woven into the same tapestry of life.

Why is it important for everyone, and especially, Empaths and Highly Sensitive People, to ground themselves through the 10th Chakra?

Empaths and HSP's need regular grounding and solidifying into their physical bodies. Because we work daily with unseen energies and tend to absorb them (even with rock solid boundaries,) it is necessary to continually reinforce our human, physical aspect.

Many Empaths, Light-workers, and spiritually inclined people wish to escape their human container and 'reality' in the belief that the body is an encumbrance to their spiritual ascension.

But this creates a lot of problems and blockages in the other chakras because we incarnated with the specific intent to be human; therefore, being chronically ungrounded, (floating in the ether) is a pathway to depression, dissolution about one's purpose, chronic pain, and illness.

Connecting to the 10th chakra with the intent of empowering one's physical incarnation leads to harmony and vibrancy on all other chakra levels.

The 10th chakra embodies:

- *The energy of the earth*
- *Balancing of the divine feminine and masculine aspect*
- *Connection to the Elemental Kingdom - Fey, crystals*
- *Remembering talents, gifts, and wisdom from previous lives*
- *Connection to Ancestors*
- *Synchronicity and Creativity*
- *12 strand DNA activation*
- *Symbiotic relationship between Light and Dark, as the 10th and 12th chakras are directly linked. They mirror each other in a similar way that Twin Flames do on their soul journey.*

As much as this chakra is earthy and dark, it actually amplifies light.

Earth elements that may be used to support the 10th chakra are any black stones such as **Hematite, Black Onyx, Black Tourmaline, Lava rock, Shungite**, as well as **Amber (fossil), Jasper**, and, **Clear Quartz** to amplify those stones.

I also like to use essential oils during meditation or in my every day with the 10th chakra, such as **Cedarwood, Frankincense, Sandalwood, Patchouli, Vanilla** and **Balsam**.

THE MEDITATION

A common way of grounding is to pull energy down from crown chakra to the root and then leave it at that. It is necessary, however, to afterward bring that grounding back up through the body to fortify all the chakras with earth energy. The stillness and rootedness are then in harmony with spirit and can be offered back to the Universe. As above, so below. Alchemy of the soul. You can record this meditation first and play it back as needed.

1. Sit in a chair or on a meditation cushion with feet planted firmly on the ground.

2. Spend a few moments in gratitude for the earth which supports you and the life you came to live.

3. Think of a place on earth that is special to you. This may be a place you have visited this or another lifetime or wish to go to in the future. It may be your garden space, or the local park or any patch of earth that brings you joy.

4. Take three deep breaths in and out, releasing tension and breathing in peaceful harmony, allowing your thoughts to settle, and observing quietly how they dissipate. Don't judge any of those thoughts, just observe and allow them to pass through.

5. Imagine reaching your energy high above you into the cosmos and bringing that star energy down. Allow it to fill the 12th chakra very slowly. When you are ready, let it filter down through the 11th, the 9th, then the 8th. This light resonating with the fullness of your Inner Being.

6. Opening your crown chakra like a lotus flower in bloom, allow that spirit infused light to fill every nook and cranny of your brain. Let it nourish your Third Eye, awakening Intuition, your throat, awakening Truth. Let it illuminate your neck and shoulders, embrace your heart chakra, your whole chest, and your arms down to your fingertips.

7. Slowly, slowly, slower yet, let this light fill your Solar Plexus, awakening Personal Power, your lower abdomen, your legs, and your root chakra in waves of radiating, empowering, light. Let this light power your soul and creativity.

8. Allow yourself time to truly relax and enjoy this process, to fill up and fuel up. Take as long as you wish, there is no time limit on this meditation. Let this be a retreat into your stillness. Remember your desire to visit the earth in a human body and embrace the journey you are on. You are a magical being on a purpose-filled mission.

9. From the bottom of your feet, imagine the ground opening beneath you, allowing you to find the earth's comforting, unconditional embrace. Surrender to the love of the Great Mother. Feel her

compassion. Feel her wisdom. Find a path among the roots of the Tree of Life. In the Underworld, there is full acceptance of your unique journey on the earth.

10. Deeper, deeper, deeper yet. Make yourself a nest among the roots, line it with soft moss, feel the warmth of your safe place. Breathe slowly. Notice the scent of forest, leaves and soil. Notice now that you are growing roots as well. These roots spread wide and deep into the earth beneath you. You are grounded in the womb of the Goddess.

11. You feel supported and seen. You can now bring this feeling of rootedness and grounding up through your feet to center your base chakra. As you bring this peaceful, rooted energy up through your 7 chakras, they begin to spin clockwise in perfect harmony with each other and your purpose on earth.

12. You feel incredibly strong of heart. You feel loved and accepted and in turn love and accept others.

13. Offer this rootedness to flow upward into the cosmos as an offering. Place your hands on the ground and feel the 'earth' beneath you. Share words of gratitude for the Great Mother. Rub your hands briskly together in front of your heart center. Feel the warmth. Keeping your hands in prayer mudra, raise them to your third eye.

What Are Your Personal Archetypes?

Everyone has personal archetypes which reveal their purpose and are the seeds from which we expand into full embodiment during each incarnation.

We experience our incarnations simultaneously, although we are taught that they progress linearly. We draw from all our incarnations to bring our specific gifts to the world.

In this exercise, you will engage Intuition to discover and remember your personal archetypes.

In your meditation space, however you wish to create that - may be in the traditional way, or sitting with back against your favorite tree, or in a cafe with a delicious coffee and pastry - journal all the archetypes which you feel you are embodying during this lifetime. You will notice that some are in seed form, some emerging, some fully awoken.

Example: Some of my archetypes are Creative, Earth Keeper, Priestess, Rebel, Revolutionary, Bridge Between Worlds, Explorer, Witch, Old Soul, Community Builder, EcoActivist.

Write all that come to heart for you. Be bold! Don't edit. Let it free flow. There may be 5 or 40.

Some will feel comfortable, some may be joyful, some fearful, some will make you laugh out loud. 'Performer' made me laugh, for instance. Not comfortable at all, and yet...

In the months to come, you can come back to this exercise and see in which ways you have grown, embodied, expanded, run away from, etc. The ones that induce fear are the ones which will help you step into full embodiment as you face that shadow.

Where do you feel joy as you explore your archetypes?
These are the juicy places of your being that are alive
within you now and you are ready to dive into deeply.

We can heal our wounds
by listening to each other's stories.

Summary

PRACTICING FULL EMBODIMENT

Journal all I Am statements which seem relevant to you at this time.

Add an item to your altar which will help you with base chakra alignment.

Choose a meditation or yoga practice which seems supportive of your journey.

Journal any thoughts which reflect ways in which you have or have not found full embodiment in your life. Does this reflect in your ability to connect to your life purpose?

What role did your mother play in helping you to find your solid footing and self-esteem and in which ways did she hinder you? Do you have any new insights now on how you will take responsibility for your own grounding and centering?

Are you able or hopeful to take your full place on Earth, taking up all the space you require?

EXPLORE YOUR ARCHETYPES

Do the 10th Chakra meditation and practice grounding strategies.

Meeting Your Mother-Line

Mother wound is infused with fear of our own power, with our mother's fear of her power, and her mother's fear. When we rise from the waters of our own fears, we slay the dragons of our mother-lines' past. We heal many generations to come.

*Relate to your mother, not as your inner child,
but as an adult. Watch the dynamic between you shift
dramatically and the doors to healing open.*

Ancestral Healing and Reconciliation

Who is she? Who am I? Who were they? Who are we?

These four questions form the basis of the exploration into your mother-line. We are connected womb-to-womb, dream-to-dream, hope-to-hope, life-to-life, and often, wound-to-wound.

Why should we dig beyond ourselves to heal mother wound?

Every woman, grandmother, mother, daughter, craves to be seen. Exploring our mother line is much like travel to another culture. It opens our eyes to experiences beyond our own. It also allows previous generations and the women who came before us to be witnessed while observing ourselves within that ancestral tapestry.

We are all connected through the alchemy of DNA, blood, and embryonic fluid in which we all floated and steeped. Many wombs have supported us through centuries of births and re-births.

We live all our lives, past, present, and future at once, and while difficult to understand that concept of over-lapping time, it allows us an idea of just how important our shadow work is: we heal all layers, our ancestors, ourselves, and our children, when we walk through the fires of personal transformation.

GATHERING STORIES

Our stories and the stories of women across the ages can empower a shift in human consciousness. These stories have been stored in our collective memory, so often snuffed out as women's voices have been silenced.

What is so important is that we give voice to ourselves and to the women before us?

Before we can do that, we must know who those women were, and how we came to grow from their experience and their ancestral wombs.

As much as we are individuals, we are also part of the clan. Like wolves, women intuitively understand that connections keep us safe, alive and in tune with the greater world in which we live. To know our mother-line is to tap into a deeper knowing of ourselves and the Great Mother. She lives and breathes through us all.

Project Big or Small

1. What is your personal mother-line?
   In your journal, detail the previous four women with whom you are connected womb-to-womb.

   > Who were they?
   > Where did they live?
   > Did you know them through stories or personal experience?
   > Do you see threads in the tapestry which lead back to you?
   > Do you look like any of them, do you share any similar traits or experiences?
   > Do you have the same love languages?

2. Add something to your altar to represent them. If you own something that has been passed down, add it, or even wear it (such as a piece of jewelry).

3. Is it possible to find more stories?
   Are there questions that need answering?
   Can you find those answers?

4. Remain here or let this ignite a journey into your personal Tree of Life.

   Do a DNA test to understand your ancestry in more detail.
   Create a family tree in your journal or as a bigger project.

   Who was she? Who am I? Who are we as a collective?

   When we see ourselves through the lens of the women who came before us, we can begin to heal what flows through us consciously.

Connected Through ancient Roots - Creating Intentional Ancestral Reconciliation

1. Write a statement of intention to witness your mother-line in its truth, and in turn to see yourself in your truth.

   Honor the stories in your statement, some of which are yours, some theirs, some uplifting, some dark.

   Honor your own journey and stories.
   Honor the roots and the new branches growing.

2. Add photographs, drawings, artifacts, or pressed tree leaves to support your statement.

3. Find a grandmother tree to meditate and heal with. Receive from her love and nurturing. Grow deep roots with her. Give to her a gift of poem, song, crystal, shell, feather, dance, or whatever springs from your heart.

4. Journal any transformation, dreams, or insights through this reconciliation.

ANCESTOR TAROT SPREAD

1. Lay your tarot or oracle cards face down one to seven as you intuitively pull them.

2. Turn them over and attune to the cards.

3. Ask these questions, or any that you imagine.

    a. What is your name and your relationship to me?
    b. What life lessons can you help me with?
    c. What wisdom do you have for me today?
    d. What sign will you use to signal your presence?
    e. What gifts have you passed on to me?
    f. How can I honor my ancestors more?
    g. How can I become a better ancestor?

4. Listen for the answers, trust what comes through, write it down, add to it the meaning or message of the card itself.

5. Thank your ancestor for their messages and wisdom.

"The story of all mothers and daughters is the story of their estrangements and their reunions."

Demetra George

Birthing Authenticity and Your Sacred Path

By choosing to be responsible for our own joy, we release Mother from being who she could not be.

If our experience has been that we made ourselves small in order to be loved, if we had denied our own authenticity in order to feel safe or accepted, it is our sacred responsibility to love, nurture and initiate ourselves into a life of Self-worth.

A woman who feels unsafe, unheard and unseen, may sacrifice her child in the same way she felt sacrificed. She may ask her, through conscious and unconscious ways, to abandon her truth.

1. In which ways did your mother or mother figure extinguish your fire?

2. Where in your body do you feel her abandonment?

3. In which life situations do you see this denial of Self re-enacted by your own actions or decisions?

    It is common with Mother Wound to practice self-aggression and self-wounding when clarity is lacking. To gain clarity, we explore the pattern initiated by our mother line.

4. Write an intention to love, nurture and initiate yourself into your authentic truth and life, to recognize yourself as worthy of expressing all of who you are and to love and nurture yourself in your uniqueness.

    Allow space for your mother to be herself as you would have wanted her to honor your space. Allow space to grieve the Mother you never had, the 'real' mother who did not materialize. Letting go of the fantasy mother we expected, we become empowered.

Notice the space that opens in your story when you release the mother you hoped for and accept the experience you had as a path to self-mastery.

Grieving the 'real mother' and taking responsibility for our own sacred, authentic path re-frames the story and shifts the focus from victim/blame to aligned co-creation.

What would you like to create in your life?

A Ritual for Releasing the Fantasy Mother

1. Write a thank you note to the fantasy mother role which Mother could not fill.

2. Feel all the places where this fantasy mother resides in your body or emotions.

3. Place this letter on your altar and honor the feelings which rise when you think of letting her go.

4. In a safe container, a cauldron on your altar or elsewhere, burn this letter with the intention of opening healing space where she once resided.

5. Scatter 'Her' ashes in a place that feels supportive, a body of moving water is best, or to the wind in your favorite place in nature.

   Create boundaries in your thoughts, speech and actions which do not invite her to materialize again, but instead fill the space with a journey onto your sacred path and highest embodiment.

"The true meaning of forgiveness is not to forget what has happened to you, but to stop wishing it had been different."

Toko-pa Turner, Belonging Book

Summary

Explore your mother line and honor it on your altar and in your journal as an act of connection and reconciliation.

Consider researching your extended family tree and witnessing the wombs which birthed your personal Tree of Life.

Create new pathways for loving and launching yourself into the life you are meant to live. Dig deep into your authenticity.

Release the 'fantasy' mother.

Stages of Grief Within Mother Wound

If we look deep enough, we can find stories of resilience and courage within any mother.

Abandonment and Grief

We may not realize it, but at the root of our mother wound lies *abandonment*. It is deeply embedded with fear. Our whole process of bonding with life, with ourselves, finding trust and safety depends on the bond we create with our mother.

No matter when our mother wound is created, during childhood or adulthood (as when mother passes or becomes unstable, slips into Alzheimer's, or suddenly becomes someone we can no longer feel safe around), a cycle of grief becomes our teacher.

The purpose of grief is to soften us, although it may seem the opposite. It, like the Great Mother, moves through seasons.

We may be grieving without consciously putting a label on it. It may feel like depression or sadness, it may be an illness or a complete collapse of immunity. We may circle it for months or years until it speaks its name. And then one day, aha, grief drops its veil and we see our manifested relationships and circumstances as our dance with her.

Abandonment and grief sometimes show up in:

*Feelings of **loss**, at times inexplicable or undefined.*
*Feelings of **disappointment** in how life has turned out.*
*Feelings of **insecurity or self-doubt**, lost sense of Self.*
*A **disconnection** with one's soul blueprint.*
*A lingering **melancholy** in body and spirit.*
***Fear** of the future or of the everyday, procrastination of 'getting on' with life.*
***Self-sabotage** - just when one begins to feel supported by life and the Universe (this may present itself as unavoidable circumstances that just seem to pop up.)*

The Outer-child engages in patterns which mirror the original abandonment of the Inner-child and creates a cycle of self-abandonment

Recognizing the patterns and clues of grief is step one. Conscious awareness of the stages allows for holding grief with love and compassion and embracing one's journey without judgement.

Shock: Realization of what is happening or has happened (this may surface years after actual trauma)
Denial: Resisting the reality, avoiding the inevitable
Anger: Outpouring of bottled-up emotions, or violence/self-destructive behavior from suppressed anger
Bargaining: Seeking for a way out of the situation in vain. Justification of circumstances
Depression: Final sinking into the reality, feeling hopeless. Tasting the pain. Self-wounding
Testing: Seeking realistic solutions. Hopeful
Acceptance: Finding the way forward
Compassion and Forgiveness: Accepting responsibility for one's own experience and healing. Releasing the need to blame. Finding compassion and forgiveness for self and mother
Integration into Wholeness: Re-connection with soul's blue-print, transformation, peace in the face of reality

"I have been/am grieving" is a simple yet powerful statement which brings clarity and brings us back to a still point with Mother Wound.

It is also important to know that grief may not follow any pattern at all, we may sink and rise back and forth through the 'stages'. Allow yourself space to grieve in your own unique way.

Monika Carless

In Mother Wound We Grieve

The mother we did not have or the mother we lost.
The bonds we did not form.
The parts of ourselves which weren't loved.
Our Inner Child's pain.
Our younger self.
The conversations we had or did not have.
The unhealed parts of Self.
The experiences which brought trauma.
The life we did not have, due to initial or self-wounding.
The words we did not hear.
The embraces not received.
Being misunderstood.

Add to this list to express your own personal grief.

Chakra Correspondences

Grief is experienced through the chakras with color (not chronological.)

Anger - Red - Root Chakra
(Frustration and resentment can become embedded here.)

Denial - Purple/Indigo - Third Eye
(refusing to see what is)

Bargaining - Blue – Throat
(self-expression, asking for what we need, often in vain)

Depression - Black - 10th Chakra - below our feet
(earth/grave, tasting the wound)

Testing - Yellow/Orange - Sacral/Solar Plexus
(searching for *realistic* solutions)

Acceptance, Compassion, and Forgiveness - Green - Heart Chakra
(a way forward)

Integration into Wholeness - White – Crown
(connection with Self, Soul's Blueprint, Oneness with Great Mother and Universe)

Use these stones for altar work, to use in healing rituals, and/or to wear as allies.

10th Chakra: Black Onyx, Black Tourmaline, Obsidian, Black Pearl, Hematite

Root: Agate, Bloodstone, Garnet, Ruby, Smoky Quartz

Third Eye: Opal, Lapiz Lazuli, Sodalite, Indigo Sapphire

Throat: Aquamarine, Turquoise, Chalcedony, Kyanite, Blue Lace Agate

Solar Plexus: Amber, Tiger's Eye, Citrine, Agate, Yellow Topaz, Carnelian

Heart: Jade, Emerald, Rose Quartz, Aventurine, Carnelian, Jasper

Crown: Amethyst, Clear Quartz, Diamond, Selenite

Sacral (Womb): Moonstone, Carnelian, Tourmaline, Amber, Citrine

Bring it to the Altar

- on the altar of your being
- on your sacred altar
- in your journal
- through your creativity: art project, song, dance, photos

Witness yourself and your grief process. In witnessing ourselves, we give ourselves permission to feel it all, to understand ourselves better, to become objective, to engage with grief in a healthy way.

1. Record the stages of grief you have experienced, which you recognize, which you are in, which are witnessed and/or healed.

2. Create a pouch or bowl of gemstones to support the chakras which need witnessing currently OR use color in other ways for the same purpose. (clothing, scarves, flowers for the altar, jewelry, candles)

3. What is your body and soul calling for now? Choose what resonates from this list or add your own ideas.

    a. a conversation with mother
    b. a self-care ritual - massage, vacation, poem written to oneself, sacred bath, extended period of silence or solitude, cord-releasing ritual, etc.
    c. clearer boundaries - with mother, in other relationships, with your own thoughts and patterns
    d. a commitment to purpose
    e. an intention for a way forward, making a clear choice

What ideas did you come up with?

Summary

Explore the stages of grief in your life. If this is your first encounter with grief as it pertains to your mother-wound, speak out loud that you have been grieving - give it voice and breath.

Give space to what you have been grieving. Add to the list suggested or create your own in your journal. This will give visual essence to where the work still is.

Use gemstones to assist with releasing grief from chakras. They can be used in meditation, worn as jewelry, carried in a pouch, held in the hands, laid on the body or on your altar.

Honor the healing process or rituals which your soul and body are calling for. Do you have a statement of purpose, a way forward that you are willing to commit to? If so, write this down.

There must be enough safety and love among women and within society for them to grieve their sadness, rage, and losses. Repressed, it gets passed on to the next generation – daughters who become mothers, who birth daughters and sons. Each generation must own their own pain and healing.

Releasing Generational Bonds
AND SUPPORT FOR YOUR INNER CHILD

Becoming happens when we allow ourselves
to be the very thing that was suppressed in us
by mother, by society, by patriarchy, and by our
own fear of loss and abandonment.

MOTHER WOUNDS ARE SOUL-TRIBE WOUNDS

Your Soul Tribe consists of anyone who has incarnated to participate in this lifetime's lessons for self-mastery and soul-evolution with you.

They include those you are related to, those with whom you are in romantic relationships, your entire family, your family's ancestors, your whole family tree, friends, co-workers, seemingly random run-ins, affairs, children lost to death (illness, accident, abortion, miscarriage, violence), relatives by law. A soul tribe can number in the thousands.

Did you know that your Inner Child has been/is in relationships with everyone in your soul tribe? She is too young to understand the complexities of your adult life and does not have the tools to process all that you have lived until this very day. She is the part of you which remains a child, bearing the gifts of youth, innocence, and naivety from which you can draw daily.

You can help her feel safe, held, heard, and protected. She is an integral part of who you are. Through releasing generational wounds, you offer her a space where she can trust again and feel valued. You offer her the support you may have not received as you developed into womanhood.

Through addressing and releasing generational bonds, you can offer your Inner Child a powerful re-set and freedom from the pain-body of those generations. This release will be felt all along the vibrational frequency of many lives. Her and your Mother Wound are part of this wider wounding. The work you commit to with this ritual may awaken connections, there may be dreams, memories or unexpected communication from others in your soul tribe. Everything that happens, serves you and your human/spiritual evolution and is neither good nor bad... it simply is.

Naming Twelve Core Soul-Tribe Wounds – Ritual

* You will perform this ritual **once** for **all** the times you have been incarnated, including all your experiential bonds in this lifetime. *

Limiting Beliefs, Violence, Poverty, Rage, Addiction, Betrayal, Abandonment, Loss of Culture, Illness, Loss of Sovereignty, Suppression of Identity, Degradation of Human Rights

The ritual intention encompasses the bathing of these 12 core wounds with Love, Compassion and Forgiveness.

1. Prepare

* Set an intention for your ritual. Keep it simple. Write it down in your journal.
ex: My intention for this ritual is to release myself from all generational bonds as experienced through my interactions with my present and past soul tribes.

 * Take a cleansing bath with any allies you feel drawn to. Crystals, candles and altar items beside your bath/shower, essential oils, bath salts, etc.

2. Create Ritual Space

* Choose a place where you feel safe and protected. This may be indoors or out.

* Gather everything you need: your written intention, your written ritual mantra, your journal, a drink to offer the Goddess/Gods you call in (and for your!), what you wish to wear, any special items you would like to bring into space (drum, rattles, pictures of ancestors, music, a ribbon for cutting bonds, etc.) There is no wrong way to do this. This is your experience to create as you wish. You might want to keep your ritual space very sparse. Listen to your intuition.

- If using a ribbon, label one end as 'I Am Free', and the other as 'All Bonds, Trauma, Dis-ease'

3. Open the Ritual

* Light candles, incense, or a fire if you have access to creating one.

* Call in the Four Directions and Four Elements and any allies/angels/goddesses/spirit guides whose energy you may want or need. (Mine is spirit of Raven, Coyote, Hummingbird, Lilith, Diana, Rowan, Holly and Oak as my staples, for example.) Feel the energy rise as you remain present to all who gather with you.

* Invoke protection and clarity by simply asking them to assist you.

* Be mindful of any shifts in wind, energy, or emotions. And...breathe.

4. The Mantra

* Visualize your soul tribe. You do not need to have faces, names or be able to imagine them *all* individually. *The intention is enough.* Picture the energetic cord of light which is your personal matrix flowing with love and compassion. There is no need to hand karma back between generations or worry about which karma belongs in which place. That no longer matters. We are clearing bonds from pure heart space where there is no separation. This ritual operates with the energy of Unity Consciousness.

* Use this as is or as a template for your own wording. Speak your mantra aloud.

Today, I act in sovereignty over my physical, emotional, intellectual, and spiritual bodies with the intention of releasing myself (present, younger, and future self) from all generational bonds created through all lifetimes, and all soul groups with whom I've experienced life on Earth. With a vibration of pure, unconditional love, compassion, and forgiveness, I release myself from all undesired bonds with others, their intentions, known and unknown toward me, setting us free from all vows, contracts, energetic cords, and dis-ease, releasing to the cosmos across all realities, dimensions, and layers of personal perceptions. I claim back to myself all soul and heart fragments lost to me through all relationships, across every generation, across all time. I send healing to all in my lineage. I release myself from all effects of previous trauma and trauma passed on through the generations. I claim protection over myself and mine and ask that any ancestors who may still be trapped in their own trauma find peace through their angels and guides. Through this I am whole, I am sovereign, and free—fully in my power, responsible for all aspects of my Self. As above, so below, as within so without. And so, it is!

(cut ribbon at this time if using)

* Observe how you are feeling in your body, take time to feel and release all tears, emotions, physical sensations.

5. Close the Ritual

* Thank the Four directions, Four Elements, angels, guides, goddesses, allies for assisting you in this powerful and **permanent shift**. Offer a libation to the Goddess who has assisted you. When you feel she has drunk, drink in celebration with Her.

* Journal any or all insights, messages, or visions. Meditate, dance or sing. Blow out your candles **when ready to return to this realm**.

* Take the day to rest and connect with the Great Mother. She has witnessed your transformation.

Congratulations!
You have created more peace, love, and unity within
yourself, within the world and all of Consciousness.

I Am

a child of the Universe and the great mother,
a spirit having a human experience.
Home is an integral part of me.

Support for Your Inner Child

An Exercise in Self-Worth

- Read to her, perhaps your favorite childhood stories.
- Surprise her with a gift that will remind her and YOU how special you both are.
- Adventure together. Play is an important aspect of joy.
- Include her in your altar, your prayers, and your daily meditation.
- Play music she may enjoy. Think about what will bring warm, safe memories for you both.
- Share a treat. Sit down at your favorite cafe and indulge in something decadent. No calorie counting, neither of you need permission to do as you please.
- Listen to her. Let her express herself in your journal, your art, and the way you live your life.
- Hold her. She loves warm blankets, cups of hot cocoa, and literal hugs. Make a habit of hugging yourself, breathe out, and enjoy the comfort of being held.
- Dream with her. Ask her what she hoped for as she grew. Let her know that her dreams are valid by pursuing any that call to you.
- Teach her about compassion, forgiveness, and living through the heart. She is always listening, watching, and learning. Help her grow strong and confident by making the choices which empower you.
- Love her. Tell her often! She never gets tired of positive affirmation.

Your relationship with your Inner Child is your relationship with the world. It is your sacred responsibility as well as a gift to yourself.

Inner child learns from Higher Self.

You can re-parent and support your inner child through the wisdom of your present self and support your present self through the wisdom of your higher self. In this way, the energetic portal between Higher self and Inner child is activated and accessed.

Summary

Visualize and become aware of your Soul - Tribe. Create an intention to release yourself from generational bonds. Meditate on what it will mean in your life, and the lives of thousands who have been journeying with you over centuries.

What are you Soul - Tribe Wounds? Can you see how the trauma of human history has resulted in your own Mother Wound?

Perform the 'Releasing Generational Bonds' Ritual. Record the time, date, and what you felt. Keep a record of anything that happened because of it.

Honor Your Inner Child. Observe how doing so creates new patterns in your life and how this releases you further from Mother Wound, into a life of your own creation.

*Women in competition with each other is a sign
of mother wound, and the generational, patriarchal
belief that we can't trust each other or even more
precisely, trust ourselves.*

Support your inner mother the same way you would support your Inner Child. Witness her with compassion and acceptance. Allow her to grieve, cry, and release. Support her with acts of kindness towards yourself. Inner child, Inner Mother, and you are one.

Shamanic Soul Journey

Sometimes we need to go deeper,
past the psyche, to the seat of the soul.

Igniting Forgiveness

Meeting Your Inner Child and Mother in a Reconciliation Fire Ritual

In this guided journey, travel to meet yourself at any stage
of your life, past, present or future.
Meet ancestors, spirit guides, animal totems, loved ones
(including pets), angels, archetypes or Inter-planetary
Beings.

The Guided, Shamanic Journey is a safe and sacred
container within which you can:

Speak to your younger or future self.
Speak to anyone with whom you have unresolved conflicts.
Remove energetic cords to completed relationships.
Obtain guidance/wisdom from ancestors or spirit guides.
Release core wounds from cell memory.
Clear vows and energetic bonds.
Facilitate compassion, empathy, emotional healing and
forgiveness.
Convey messages to loved ones on the Other Side.
Address Mother, Father, Sibling or Partner Wound.
Access Intuition and your Inner Wise One.

*The Guided Shamanic Journey allows for alchemical
shifts within your soul's evolution.*

* This ritual is to meet Inner Child and Mother but can also
be used to meet with other people/entities in your life, and
as such this ritual can be re-used many times for different
applications.

1. Find a comfortable place where you can sit in meditative state.

2. Arrange your surroundings to support the magical experience you are about to enter. Light candles to invite angelic and spirit messengers. Apply essential oils of your choice if you wish to your pulse points. You can use these to bring comfort to you during the journey. Pull a card or two and set on your altar. Have your journal ready by your side. You will want to record this very important step in your transforming mother wound journey.

3. Set an intention for your journey. You can write it down and place on your altar as well.

4. Silence and put away phone.

5. Journey in silence or with supportive music.

6. Sit now with your body in an alert but comfortable position.

7. Take and release three deep breaths. Breathe three breaths of unconditional love and peace. Release all anxiety, fear, and judgement. Breathe in three more breaths of love. Breathe our love, sharing it with the consciousness.

8. Close your eyes and begin.

9. Find yourself in your body, a safe, warm environment where you feel completely at ease. You will notice a path to follow to your left and further down the path, a set of stairs which will take you to a deeper part within yourself. Take these steps at a leisurely pace, each one taking you further away from this realm, and into a realm where anything is possible. You are no longer in the 3rd. Dimension but in the dimension of your Heart Chakra.

Your body is filled with light, and you are now a boundless sea of beingness. You are home.

10. What is your name in this realm? Answer from your Higher Self. Allow any of your inter-dimensional names to surface.

    You can begin recording in your journal now, knowing that you remain in the dimension of the heart chakra, even as you write and look around.

11. Invite in any of your guides, angels, animal familiars or a mentor whom you wish to guide you on the journey. What is/are their names?

12. Look around and describe what the heart chakra feels like or looks like. What colors do you see? What sensations do you feel here?

    Feel everything fully. Allow raw emotions to surface. Do not edit how you feel. It is safe here to feel. You will be viewing the story of what was but not engaging with the drama of it. Remember, you are not in mind/ego space. You are in heart space.

    In this vast, warm, supportive space, notice how old you are. Write that down. This may be your present self or at any age.

13. Ask your mentor/guide or animal familiar if present to assist you in lighting a fire and place some seats around it in a sacred circle.

    Pick a memory from your childhood or some other time and invite your Younger Self and Mother to join you in this circle. Ask any other people you wish to also see at the fire to join you now.

Take note of where they choose to sit, how old they are, what they are wearing, anything that seems important to you at this time. You may wish to have your Younger Self to sit near you, hold their hand, offer a hug. Greet Mother with your most honest emotions in this moment.

14. Let the memory play out on in your mind's eye, knowing that all at the fire can also see this memory. You are not re-living it; you are simply observing.

    According to the story you let play out on the screen, you can have a conversation with Mother. Ask her anything you need to know and let her answer. Feel your feelings fully as you do this, breathe into it, experience it.

    Allow Mother to feel what you are feeling, to see things from your point of view. She will come to understand you in a way she could not have before, or in ways you could not share before.

    Remember, you are here as a vast and boundless energy of pure, unconditional love. Record anything your Higher Self may have to say during this experience.

    You can step into Mother's heart now to feel what she's feeling as she fully understands your suffering. Allow compassion to wash through you. Through this, you can experience *the best part of Mother, had she known better.* Record what she is feeling as she experiences your previous pain.

    Knowing that Mother was probably doing the best she could with the resources she had at the time, what does Mother have to say about the pain you felt then? *Let her say everything that is on her heart.*

What does your Inner Child/Younger Self have to say to Mother in response? What does your Present Self have to say?

Are there any more questions you need to ask Mother. Listen for her answers. Remember she is speaking from her Higher Self not the person she was or even is today.

What would have to happen in order for you to reconcile with Mother for this particular memory or any other memories you wish to clear? After hearing from Mother at soul level, allowing her to feel your pain and witnessing her response, can you conceptualize coming to a degree of, or complete peace about the situation?

This fire ceremony does not attempt to justify Mother's actions in any way, it simply allows the two of you to meet each other in a safe, non-judgmental, heart space.

15. Reassure your Younger Self

   "You do not have to experience this pain again. I share with you all the resources I have now to help you deal with anything you may still be struggling with. I love you and will protect, guide and support you."

16. Allow everyone at the fire to dissolve into the ether.

17. Now look around the heart space again...how has the region changed around you? What sensations do you feel in your body? In your heart?

18. When you are ready, return to the present moment via the same stairs and path you took at the beginning of the ritual. Take your time to notice what the path and stairs look like now, how you are feeling.

19. Open your eyes when you are ready.

20. While you are fresh from your ritual, write a short (or long) letter to your past self. What advice does she have for your inner child?

Your ritual is over.
Please nourish your body and drink plenty of water.

The days and months to come may reveal new insights.

Blessed be.

In a shorter ritual, if you wish to return to more memories or wounds, simply create conversations around the virtual fire with Mother and Younger or present Self. Allow them to feel what you are feeling and respond from their higher self. Record the conversation and add more layers of reconciliation, until those memories no longer contain a charge for you.

From Co-Dependence to Co-Creation

Co-dependency is common in people who have suffered trauma, abandonment, loss, and abuse.

We can not only be co-dependent in our physical relationships but also with our thought patterns, resources, ideas, certain behaviors which when engaged with, give a type of dopamine effect, and keep us trapped in a cycle of self-abandonment.

Co-dependence is a loss of Self.

It happens because we become adjusted to thinking that our needs are not important, and that it is safer to tend to the moods, desires and expectations of those who control our very existence, specifically Mother, on whom we rely for appreciation, love, compassion, encouragement, and the guidance to honor our own wisdom.

To become embodied in our purpose and to be able to function from a place of empowerment, we look honestly at the places in our life where we are more attached to what others think of us, or how we can please, and instead, embrace the knowledge that *we hold all the keys to unlocking our best life.*

**When we feel unworthy,
we act from shame and guilt.**

*"I am not what happened to me.
I am what I choose to become."*

Carl Gustav Jung

Journal / Action Prompts

1. In what areas of your life can you listen to your own intuition more and recognize your own authority and sovereignty?

2. Take steps to recognize your needs, to acknowledge your own voice, and to give to yourself. There is no-one who knows what you need better than yourself.

3. You cannot spoil a child with love. Write down ten ways you can offer affection to yourself. Practice being Self-ish from a place of Self-worth.

4. We re-create our childhoods with behavior that mirrors Mother's detachment. Come back to Self. Write down some patterns you would like to break.

5. What is your truth? Create a statement/mantra that validates your reason for being on earth and being loved. *"I am here to...I deserve to...I believe that/in... I am a person of"* (list your qualities and gifts.)

6. In what ways do you give away your power/give away self? Turn those ways around now... in what ways can you restore your power?

7. List your core relationships. What boundaries do you see as being weak in those relationships? Taking responsibility for your boundaries, without apologizing for doing so, (you have every right to protect yourself), implement changes and watch yourself leap into deeper embodiment of purpose!

8. When we crave the mother we did not have, we seek substitutions in other relationships. Write down one to three things you will no longer tolerate in your life, including self-sabotaging habits.

9. A relationship with abundance/resources/money is reflected in our relationship with ourselves. "I don't need much, I never have enough, it's not important to me, or in reverse, hoarding money and not giving ourselves what we need are ways we enact shame around abundance. The core statements that we have absorbed are "I am not enough. I do not deserve. There is not enough for ME."

    Mantra: I am enough. I am abundant. I create my own resources from within. My desires are supported by the Universe.

10. Independence does not mean that we do not care for others. It means that we do not become enmeshed in their lives so far as to block their ability to *care for themselves*. Living for Self is a recognition of our own worth. A balance of these is making sure that we have a full cup before we pour for someone else. No-one can sustainably live their purpose from a place of self-deprivation.

    Mantra: I respect my authority over my own life, I am self-reliant, I love who I have become and am becoming. I give from a full well of abundance.

11. It is perfectly OK to be a giver, to be generous, as long as it is not from a place of fear or guilt. You are responsible for yourself now. You will not be abandoned if you do not give or please enough because you practice healthy boundaries with yourself and others. You will not be rejected or be expected to be perfect.

    List one way in which you have become a co-creator in your life, and have released fear, trusting that you will be safe in your decisions.

12. Connectedness is what every human being craves in
    order to self-actualize. When we face the fear of those
    dark places within ourselves, when we embrace fear
    born of being rejected, abused, abandoned, or
    neglected, we find that it can dissipate simply by being
    felt *instead of being avoided*! We get through it. We see
    that it has an end. Then, we can connect deeply to
    ourselves, to Spirit, to the Great Mother, to others,
    without losing our-Selves.

    In what ways do you feel stronger now that you have
    faced the dark shadows of Mother Wound? Celebrate
    your courage and the work you have done.

Summary

Journey to meet Mother and your Younger Self in a shamanic ritual for reconciliation. Write a letter from your Future Self to the Present You with advice from her place of future wisdom.

What may you need to forgive yourself for? Find areas of self-abandonment and write a note to yourself expressing your compassion, love, and forgiveness. Acknowledge that you did the best that you could with the tools that you had.

You have made it through many layers of shadows in these past months. Congratulations, you have done the work! You have created new pathways in your brain and heart and can see life from a place of joy and co-creation.

So much of modern parents' efforts are spent on providing material well-being, but not on the emotional and spiritual bonding with each other or their children. Often, it is that pressure of chasing perfection and material expansion—projecting our own unrealized ambitions and fears of scarcity and survival on our children—that promotes and creates the split between us and our children.

Our children do not need more toys or a bigger bedroom. They need more interaction and the ability to explore new things without attachment to outcome or <u>performance</u>. If we are always focused on the goals and trying to get our children to a certain milestone, we are missing out on what is going on with them or who they are right now. When they are not accepted for who they are, our children will go on to demand certain behaviors from their relationships, rather than accepting people for who they are. Our children do not care how young or thin we are. And yet it is our own inner struggles that prevent us from properly bonding with our children, or anyone else in our lives.

It is our own capacity to meet ourselves in compassion and unconditional love that can provide an accepting and loving environment for our children. As cruel and non-accepting as we are to ourselves is how we show up for all our relationships.

The mother preoccupied with her internal suffering is lost to the child. The children sense that their mother is elsewhere and take it personally. They then carry the grief of the loss of their mother to her sadness, to her internal preoccupations, to her anger, to her sense that her life has been stolen from her.

Motherhood is a choice that creates consequences that ripple out way beyond our own lives.

Galina Singer

One way to heal the past and future is to be here now.

Loving Self – The Feminine Mystery

EMBRACING SENSUALITY & CHAOS

We can be living in the now and healing core wounds from the past. In fact, rooted in presence is the safest way to address our story.

BEAUTIFUL EMBODIED YOU

Journal ways in which you have grown into Self - Love through exploring your Mother Wound.

- What do you think has been a pivotal moment in your quest to uncover mother-wound shadows?

- Where did you feel a shift in how you view yourself against the background of your story?

- Add to your altar something which signifies how you feel about yourself today, having done all this work.

Honoring Emotion and Chaos
STRETCHING OUR WINGS

The Divine Feminine is right brain, emotion, chaos, intuition, receiving, nurturing, surrendered to love, healing, gentle, wise, expressive, patient, flexible, creative, soft, peaceful, heart-centered, flowing, expansive, inner.

- Which of these do you feel safe expressing and being/or are already?

- Do you see them as valuable, or have they in the past been a source of vulnerability?

- Is there room in your relationship with Mother to express yourself as chaos and intuition?
  Does it feel safe, or do you have a role to play?
  What is this role?
  Can you give yourself permission to step out of your role and into your full embodiment?

- How real can you be with Mother? To express your wildness without apology?

- What parts of you do you wish you could be real about?

- What parts of yourself are you withholding from yourself? Is there anything you wish to say to yourself about who you are at your core, and give yourself permission to be?

The Divine Masculine is left brain, logic, adventure, firm, action, reason, survival, loyal, rational, strength, aggressive, mind centered, assertive, analytical, emotionally guarded, outer, planner.

- Which of these qualities do you see in yourself?

- How can you bring more balance to your inherent feminine/masculine essence?

- We are culturally conditioned to express what is thought to be gender correct, and to suppress what is thought incorrect. Have you been asked to be more of one than the other? Perhaps shamed into 'right' behaviour? How?

- In which areas of our life do you feel you need bring this balance to? What requires more of your masculine or more of your feminine?

- Balanced, do you feel more courage to assert and claim your full embodiment on Earth?

- If you were to write a letter to Mother, what would you tell her about the masks you wish to take off, or which roles you will no longer play to please her or your Inner Child. This is standing in your power, because the only validation you can be sure of being granted is the one you give yourself.

  I will no longer wear the mask of ...
  1.
  2.
  3.
  4.
  5.
  etc.

  I Am...
  1.
  2.
  3.
  4.
  5.
  etc.

Honoring Sexual Energy, Passion and Desire

Lover. Priestess of Sensuality. Creatress of Life.

Your Sexuality is the Life Force of the Universe Through Which All is Created. It is a Scared Flow of the Divine Through You. It Powers Everything You Create in Your Life.

Your Yoni and Womb are the sacred cauldrons in which all life is begun. It is a mystery how spirit and body are knit together, deep within a woman's body, and how desire and sexuality are the conduits for human incarnation. Desire is the seed of all life.

Mantras for Life

My sexuality is sacred.

I am free to express my desire and sexuality.

I adore my yoni and offer her rituals of love.

I deserve deep pleasure.

Life is pleasure.

I am pleasure.

I am turned on by life.

I honor my personal sexual preferences and explore them with freedom.

I take pleasure in life.

Desire is my birthright.

I love my body, and thank it for its service.

I am naked in my emotions.

My heart and yoni are connected through love and compassion.

My sexuality is ecstatic.

I explore my sexuality and feel empowered by my choices.

My breasts, yoni, womb are part of my sovereignty and are respected and held holy.

I am irreverent.

I am a sexual being.

My sexual energy flows through all my chakras.

Pleasure and desire are sacred.

My yoni represents the Great Mother and the Divine Feminine.

Use the yoni mudra during meditation to calm the nervous system and embrace clam and peace.

Your yoni is your energetic heart!

- *Practice yoni gazing. In worshiping the yoni, appreciating her beauty and presence, we remember our own divinity and that pleasure is our birthright.*

- *Consider using a yoni egg to connect with your sacred sexuality, to strengthen your pelvic floor, to deepen your sexual practice and your emotions around sensuality.*

- *Create a sensuality practice. You are your own best lover, most connected with your desire, your needs,*

149

*and kinks. Practicing self-love reminds the body that she is loved, respected, and appreciated. It **reclaims** your body for yourself.*

- *Embrace the wild woman within who is free of shame and condemnation for her raw impulses.*

- *Take a picture of your beautiful yoni. Consider adding to your altar or journal.*

- *Write what you love or don't love about your yoni, body, and/or sexuality. Offer a prayer to your body and sexuality forgiving yourself for any ways you may have ignored, shamed, or abused it. Offer loving-kindness to yourself for the journey you have been on, and in the knowing that you did the best you could with the understanding you had at the time.*

*"You are accepted, you are accepted forever,
just as you are"*

Osho

Summary

Balancing the Masculine with the Feminine - Taking of your masks and living in self-acceptance.

Which masks will you shed and what are you I Am statements?

Journal mantras for embracing your sexuality. Include them in your daily vocabulary

Sensuality Practice - Reconnecting with Desire

Allow wild woman to emerge and together, create new practices for your sexual pleasure.

Accept the challenge to take a photo of your yoni and add to your altar or journal or draw/paint her!

Sexuality as a prayer

Crossing the Threshold

Our joy and our sorrow can exist peacefully within us.

Wild Woman, welcome to your Emergence!

Through the process of intentionally delving into mother wound for the purpose of transmutation, we can symbolically re-enter the womb and re-birth ourselves as women aligned to purpose.

This is accomplished through Intention, the magic used by all mystics to create and manifest desired outcomes.

Our soul's greatest desire is to actualize to **purpose.**

When we find transformation through understanding Mother, accepting mother's role in our life - her gifts and limitations, when we find compassion and forgiveness for her, *we find those same things for ourselves* and open to stepping into our purpose and power.

All along, this has been the alchemical soul-shift occurring beneath healing mother wound through divine feminine wisdom.

To step into purpose is to come into embodiment as a spiritual being having a human experience.

WRITE YOUR INTENTION

1. In your journal, **write an intention** for stepping into your purpose and power. This can be one sentence or many.

    example: 'My desire is to discover the parts of myself which reveal my soul purpose, and with clear intention step into my empowerment by loving myself as I am, while seeking divine growth'

2. Let whatever wants to come flow, in your own way, your own words, they will be perfect as they are. Feel

this intention. This invites Source to co-create with you.

3. **Create a vision board** (physical or on Pinterest) of what you *FEEL* your purpose is or may be, knowing that soul-purpose evolves as you do. Share your vision board in our secret group if so inspired.

Purpose is not what we do, it is who we are.

"On my board, I have things that excite my soul, such as images of books, gardens, beautiful interior design, architecture, chickens, anything that helps me connect with what is sacred to me. The images speak of a simple life, sacred geometry, silence, wisdom. This unfolded into my purpose of being an Earthkeeper and mentor, but more importantly, being of service, which is my true purpose, no matter how I express it, professionally or personally."

EMBRACING A NEW VISION

1. Take a photo of yourself, or have someone help you, in the woods, by a stream, a field or anywhere in nature that speaks to you. Dress according to your current desire to express Self. You can be clothed or sky-clad. Close to the Great Mother, embraced by her eternal love and grace, envision the woman who has emerged through her mother-wound journey

2. Add to this photo, a revised version of your mother-wound story.

   What new perspective can you write your story from?

   How has your perspective shifted?

Often, my clients say that the story is vastly different from the one they wrote before. It is less the things that happened, itemized, or re-visited, and more a story of transformation and wisdom for themselves and others.

What pieces of YOU have been retrieved during this journey?

example: confidence, wisdom, self-trust, self-love, self-empowerment, voice

Add these insights to your story.

Abundance flows in the space created by stepping into compassion and forgiveness. Feel into the places where you have released and made room for new blessings.

3. Journal where abundance has already appeared in the months since you began your journey, and what you would like to manifest in the future from your new state of awareness.

"Every decision I make is a choice between a grievance and a miracle. I choose the miracle. When you make a choice, you change the future."

Deepak Chopra

Rebirthing into an Aligned Purpose

VISIONARY EXERCISE
A SYMBOLIC ACT OF RE-BIRTHING

Your birth was your first act of courage. To be born-again is to be present to Self, to understand ourselves in the context of the events which have shaped us, but which do not define us.

It is to release all victimhood and embrace empowerment by creating the life we wish.

Life does not happen to us. We create it with our thoughts, words, and actions.

Gather:
A long stick (can be broomstick, branch, or a sturdy string)
A bowl of salt
Sage or Palo Santo
Candles
Journal

- Cast a circle of salt into which you and the stick will fit easily. If you do not wish to use salt, you can cast an imaginary circle using your broom, athame, or finger!

- Arrange candles, crystals, and any sacred objects around the circle.

- Find music that inspires you into joy.

- Prepare by meditating and setting an intention in your journal for re-birthing into your intended purpose, health, empowerment, ease of being and soul's blueprint free of previous challenges presented by the mother wound.

- Light candles. (Be careful with fire around your clothes as you step into circle!)

- Invite all allies, ancestors, spirit guides, elements, goddesses, etc. whom you wish to accompany you in your re-birthing.

- Record in journal any emotions surfacing.

- Step into the circle, standing on one side of the stick, connect with all energies present. Take your time. There is no hurry.

- When centered, grounded, and ready, say these words as you step over the stick:

I am re-born
I am embodied
I am on purpose
I am whole
I Am

Congratulations, Wild Woman, you have birthed yourself with clear intention, empowered and responsible for your own emergence! Your life will continue to shift, focus, and stretch you. Perhaps you wish to dance now, sing, or howl!

Thank all guides/elements present for supporting you in ritual. With hands at heart center, step out of the circle and emerge Wild, Free and Embodied as you were meant to be at your birth. Record all in journal.

"The psyches and souls of women also have their own cycles and seasons of doing and solitude, running and staying, being involved and being removed, questing and resting, creating and incubating, being of the world and returning to the soul-place."

Clarissa Pinkola Estés

Summary

Emergence: Write an Intention for stepping into your power.

Create a vision board and FEEL into your purpose.

Take a photo of yourself as Wild Woman, Free and Empowered.

Re-write all or parts of your story/or add to, with the perspective of having delved into Mother Wound. What pieces of Self have you retrieved through your work?

Record where abundance has or is showing up in your life due to your commitment to heal Mother Wound.

Crossing the Threshold - A re-birthing exercise. Congratulations, Wild Woman!

Closing Prayer

Great Mother
Thank you for the gifts of birth and re-birth.
For your healing touch, your embrace, your guidance.
Thank you for the gifts of your womb –
the knowing that I am Creatress,
Alchemist, and birther of my own reality.
May I remember the wisdom of my mother-line,
and take the medicine of my experiences to create
transformation for myself and others.
When we heal, we become the healer.
Teach me which lessons to pass on
and which to let fall away.
My voice carries the song of my ancestors,
the women who came before me.
May my voice ring true for the generations ahead of me.
May my song echo the ancient stories of all woman-kind.
May my heart be filled with love and compassion for all
mothers, including myself.
May we all rise, hand in hand,
stronger for the journey of our lifetimes.
We rise in gratitude.
And so, it is.

Moving Forward with Pachamama
A Magical Shamanic Practice

Flowers, trees, weeds, roots, and fruits contain healing codes which over the centuries have become discovered and applied by wise women, shamans, and practitioners of natural healing.

Essential Oils are powerful allies which can be engaged with during meditation, in a grounding/centering practice, or to release stuck emotions.

Wearing the 'spirit' of the plant is a way of communicating directly with the Great Mother. It is a way of energetically being comforted by Her and experiencing her love.

Use only the highest quality oils, not only for the best healing potential, but also to honor the plants in the way they are grown, harvested and prepared.
*Sustainability in essential oil production is paramount

Magical Practice

Choose 1 to 12 plant essences to work with for the next year. To commit one year to a magical practice is to commit yourself to a year of intentional creativity and manifestation. It will affect other areas of your life including a deeper awareness of purpose and soul evolution.

Add to your mother wound journal or another separate one (can be online journal);

- name and image of plant (including Latin name)
- its spiritual association/healing gift (what it is used for)
- any history you wish to explore (ex: rose has a very ancient applications and meanings)

- what it means to you and how your relationship with this plant spirit has developed
- any magical synchronicities or healing due to your work with this plant?
- how do you feel when you smell the aroma? What emotions come up?
- begin and end work with each plant with a prayer of gratitude

An alternative is becoming a Tree Mother and working with twelve trees instead of oils.

*I am safe to be in my fullness
and take up all the space I need in the world.
I am safe to pursue the path I envisioned, desired,
and trained for before I incarnated.
The whole of the Universe, my guides and
my ancestors support me on my journey.
I embody my purpose.*

Shadow work is a practice
It's a devotion
A system of self-assessment
It's not just tears and dark nights
It not just calls upon Hekate and Lilith
It is so much more than entropy and pain
It is that extra filter we installed so we can check into our
empathy before judging
It's the insights into your painful childhood that hit you
while doing dishes
The extra breath you take while stuck in traffic
to find your center
I do not discourage your wails
The altars you're called to create
The way Kali or Yemayá burns in your blood
I welcome it all
But it's so much more
It's devotion to our truth
Remembrance of who came before us
It's finding your humble
It's holding the child you were
Honoring the teen within who fought to be heard
And making space for the lessons as well as the pain felt
It's the light within that shines
And the darkness that heals
It's a promise to oneself that says
"I will not be ignorant of my own ways "
It is awareness

Jesica Nodarse

About the Author

Monika Carless is a globally published author and mentor to Earthkeepers, Witches and Creatives. She lives a quiet life on Vancouver Island focused on simple pleasures with her partner of many moons. Her heart song is guiding women to their sovereignty and fearless authenticity. Especially interested in archetypes, myths and life mastery through self-healing practices, Monika mines wisdom from cronedom and the healing powers of art and words.

Moon Oracle posts and daily inspiration can be found on Instagram @monikacarless

Books: The Dark Pool Trilogy, Healing Mother Wound Course Book, and Tessa and the Faeries are available on Amazon, Barnes and Noble, Indigo Books

Photo by Sara Deyell

Work with Monika: Connect via monikacarless.com

Contributors

Many thanks to the following authors for their contribution to this course book. Please take a moment to check out more of their work via the links below.

Sarah Norrad ~ sarahnorrad.com
Galina Singer ~ galinasinger.com
Sophie Gregoire - ~ sophiegregoire.com
Tanya Markul ~ tanyamarkul.com
Jesica Nodarse ~ facebook.com/heathenwordsmith

Teachers to Explore

Throughout the book, you will find quotes from many amazing teachers. I encourage you to check out each of them.

Sharon Blackie
Henry David Thoreau
Clarissa Pinkola Estes
Carl Jung
Ursula K. Le Guin
Bell Hooks
Lucy H. Pearce
Demetra George
Tokopa Turner
Socrates
Pema Chödrön
Lao Tzu
Deepak Chopra

Made in the USA
Las Vegas, NV
19 July 2022